faith-filled
moments

Helping Kids See God
in Everyday Life

KELLI B. TRUJILLO

wesleyan
publishing
house

Indianapolis, Indiana

www.kellitrujillo.com

Copyright © 2009 by Wesleyan Publishing House
Published by Wesleyan Publishing House
Indianapolis, Indiana 46250
Printed in the United States of America
ISBN: 978-0-89827-406-6

Library of Congress Cataloging-in-Publication Data

Trujillo, Kelli B.
    Faith-filled moments : helping kids see God in everyday life / Kelli
Trujillo.
        p. cm.
    Includes bibliographical references and index.
    ISBN 978-0-89827-406-6 (alk. paper)
    1. Christian education--Home training. 2. Christian education of
children. I. Title.
    BV1590.T78 2009
    248.8'45--dc22
                                        2009012139

For Davis Paul, Lucia Mae, and
baby number three

contents

acknowledgments

I'm so grateful to the many people who walked with me on the journey of bringing this book to life.

Thank you . . .

. . . to my mom-friends and their kids who tested some of my written instructions and let me know, among other things, that I'd forgotten to say "*grease* the baking sheet" . . . but ate the messed-up pretzels anyway! Thank you to Sarah Bontrager, Emily Cetola, Renee Foor, Anna Hannum, Tina Miles, Heather Pickey, and Kara Rusk.

. . . to my parents-in-law, David and Anita Trujillo, who did some pinch-hitting babysitting for me during my final week of somewhat frantic work on this manuscript.

. . . to my editor Kevin Scott, my publisher Don Cady, and the rest of the terrific folks at Wesleyan Publishing House who care deeply about helping families grow closer to Christ.

. . . to my mom for baking monster cookies, growing salt crystals, reading children's poetry, and playing endless games with me. And thank you to my dad for flying kites, building forts, stargazing, and backyard camping with me. Together you filled the everyday moments of my childhood with extraordinary wonder and ever-growing faith.

. . . to my husband, David. I knew from the moment I first met you that you'd be an amazing father. Thank you for all you do to show Jesus to our kids as you model a life of wholehearted devotion.

introduction

Everyday Life . . . Extraordinary Faith

Tapatío.

It's the classic brand of hot sauce you'll find on the table at any self-respecting authentic Mexican restaurant. It's the scrambled-egg topping loved by both my father-in-law and my husband that shocked my Midwest sensibilities. And in just six minutes, it changed my son's life.

OK, so maybe it didn't alter the very course of his life . . . but it *did* form his understanding of God's love and forgiveness in a significant way. And that sense of God's forgiveness—of how absolute and powerful and undeserved it is—will stick with him and will change him, again and again, throughout the rest of his life. And it all happened with a tarnished penny and ten drops of Tapatío.

It had been a tough day. My son had gotten in trouble several times, and his little four-year-old guilty conscience was starting to get the better of him. I told him he was forgiven, but the cloud of shame persisted. He was in a funk, and if you've got kids, you know how persistent a four-year-old funk can be!

So I remembered something I'd heard about hot sauce and pennies and we sat down together for an experiment. We examined a tarnished penny and saw how dull its color had become. Then we loaded it up with Tapatío and waited.

"Honey, you've made some bad choices today. We all sin and do things wrong," I told him. "Remember how tarnished that penny was? That's sort of like what sin does to us. It makes us 'dirty' inside."

After six minutes, we wiped the penny off and . . . *voila*! The tarnish was gone. It wasn't just clean; it looked brand new. It actually sparkled!

Wanna try this penny experiment with your child? Turn to page 80 (Moment 25) for instructions.

"Look at the penny, Bud," I said. "This is like God's forgiveness. The tarnish is gone. The penny is cleaned off, bright as new."

Then it happened. It clicked. I could see it in his eyes . . . he *got it*. The funk began to dissipate and a hint of a smile came to his eyes as he put that shiny penny into his pocket for safe-keeping. In his own little way he'd gotten a sense of God's forgiveness. He'd realized something my words couldn't communicate on their own.

It was a God-moment. It was a faith-filled moment.

And it got me thinking . . .

dreams

What do I really want for my kids? How do I want them to understand God and to learn about his truth and his world? How do I want them to relate to God and to view their faith?

What is it that *you* really want for your kids?

If your dreams are anything like mine, they may go something like this: I want my children to know God. Not just know about God, but know him. I want my children to love God. And I want my children to have a full and enduring sense through every experience life throws their way that God loves them. I want my kids to see the Bible as the essential and true guide for their lives. And I want them to really live their faith. To not just hear the Word or say the right answers but to go the extra mile, turn the other cheek, go out there, and change the world!

But here's the thing: This sort of faith doesn't just happen. And the greatest church children's ministry in the world can't accomplish this. Helping your children grow to love God? It's your job.

a big job

God didn't pull any punches when he told his people how he wanted them to live. He laid it all out, in simple pointed terms, in Deuteronomy 6:4–5: "Hear, O Israel: The LORD our God, the LORD is one. Love the LORD your God with all your heart and with all your soul and with all your strength."

The ancient Jewish understanding of loving God with all one's heart, soul, and strength was a bit different from how we view the meaning of these words today. The Hebrew word for *heart* (*lev*) communicated the idea of one's thoughts and intentions, and the word for soul (*nefesh*) referred to one's passions and desires. The phrase translated into English as "with all your strength" literally means "exceedingly" or "very, very much." In Old Testament culture, doing something with all one's "heart and soul" meant doing something "with the totality of one's thoughts, feelings, intentions, and desires."* Jesus built on this idea in Mark 12:30 when he recited Deuteronomy 6:5 and added "with all your mind" to the description of love for God, referring specifically to a person's intellectual understanding and cognitive abilities.

Though our modern understanding of what *heart, soul, mind,* and *strength* mean may vary a bit from the ancient Hebrew connotations of these words, the key idea remains the same across the centuries. The command challenges us to have a full, complete, undivided love for God. In essence, the command says, "Love God with every part of your being, with every ounce of you, with everything you've got."

But God didn't stop with his command about love in Deuteronomy 6. He went on to say,

These commandments that I give you today are to be upon your hearts. Impress them on your children. Talk about them when you sit at home and when you walk along the road, when you lie down and when you get up. Tie them as symbols on your hands and bind them on your foreheads. Write them on the doorframes of your houses and on your gates. (Deut. 6:6–9)

Impress them. I love this translation of the Hebrew, which literally means "repeat them." Our English word *impress* refers to making one's mark with a stamp or a seal. It means to change something by leaving a permanent influence or alteration. It's important for us to consider what kind of impression we make on our kids. But God calls us to something more. It's not about *our* impression on our kids but about joining him in putting *his* impression on their lives.

God . . . *everywhere*

Rather than the sad but too-often-true stereotype of Christians whose faith is segmented away into a few hours on Sunday morning, God's people are to have him front and center in their thoughts, words, and activities in every sphere of their lives and at all times. In their journeying, in their waking, in their resting, in their homes, outside of their homes, in their thoughts, in their deeds, and in the work of their hands, God is there.

So when we think about "impressing" a passionate, wholehearted love for God into our children's lives, we need to move faith outside the bounds of Sunday school or VBS or family devotion time. Though focused times of worship and learning are important, we must also strive to draw our kids' attention to God in every single part of their lives.

With a little creativity, you can cultivate in your child an enduring awareness of God's presence and turn just about *any* moment into a God-moment.

So . . .

Blowing bubbles together can be a God-moment.
Baking cookies together can be a God-moment.
Playing tag can be a God-moment.
Hunting for worms can be a God-moment.
Exploding a soda bottle can be a God-moment.

Beyond just reading, listening, or talking, God designed us to encounter him and learn about him through all of our senses—touch, smell, hearing, sight, and even taste! You can use a rich variety of multisensory experiences, such as science experiments and games and crafts and everyday routines, to draw your child closer to God.

using this book

The *Faith-Filled Moments* in this book are organized into four basic sections to help you target four crucial areas of love for God:

* Heart—ideas that zero in on emotions and draw out feelings of love for God.
* Soul—ideas that help your child connect with God through spiritual-growth habits.
* Mind—ideas that focus on the intellectual side of faith, such as learning Scripture and theological concepts.
* Strength—ideas that help your child put his love for God into action.

You can start at the beginning of the Heart section and work your way through the ideas, focusing on each aspect of devoted love for God. Or you can flip to the *Faith-Filled Moments* Finder at the end of the book to navigate the ideas yourself. It's a glorified index of sorts that will point you to the ideas that fit your child best. There are lots of ways to find ideas there, so take your pick!

These pages are also packed with **variety**. From science experiments to cooking projects, crafts, games, and trips, you'll discover lots of diverse and surprising ways to connect your child to God. You can select an idea based on your child's natural affinities or you can prompt him to try something new and different. A quick word about safety: Some parts of the cooking projects and science experiments should only be done by an adult and, though it goes without saying, *all* of these activities should be supervised.

Remember that these ideas are designed to be **flexible**. You can do them with one child or twelve, with preschoolers or preteens. Each one includes spiritual insights and several exploration questions for discussion. With older kids, you can really dive into the theological concepts and discussion starters; with younger kids, just take the idea and make it really basic. My hope is that you take my suggestions, sift them through the filter of your kids' ages and interests, and decide what will work best for you.

Go **at your own pace**. This isn't meant to be an idea-per-day book. You don't want to bring a stressful pace to your family's life! Instead, decide how you want to use these ideas. You may want to try a few per week. After all, you're probably already playing games with your kids, reading with them, and preparing snacks for them. These spiritual connections can fit right in with your family's everyday life! Or you may want to take a once-a-week approach, selecting ideas in advance that will fit your family's routine on a given day. With a bunch of ideas, you can plan to try out one per week and work through this entire book!

And I want to encourage you to **mark up** this book. Make notes in the margin about ideas you really liked; circle ideas you know you want to try; jot down the dates when you completed each of the *Faith-Filled Moments*; make notes about funny, insightful, or precious things your child said as you encountered God together.

transform moments, transform lives

When you're busy sneaking spiritual growth into activities with your kids, God will also be at work sneaking in some transformation in your life and heart. You'll start to see him and sense him everywhere. You'll find your love for him growing and enlarging as you join your child in developing a loving regard for God, practicing spiritual-growth habits together, learning about God's Word, and serving him in ways that stretch you out of your comfort zone.

So grab your child by the hand and dive in. Fill each moment with faith, and together love God with all you've got!

A Word about Cooking . . .

The recipes and science experiments in this book use these abbreviations:

tsp. = teaspoon
tbsp. = tablespoon
c. = cup
oz. = ounce

note

*Jeffrey H. Tigay, *The Jewish Publication Society Torah Commentary—Deuteronomy* (Jerusalem: JPS, 1996), 77.

with all your heart : part 1

*cultivating a deep
and enduring love for God*

"God loves you."

These words are emblazoned on smiley-faced T-shirts and bumper stickers; they're the first words of evangelistic tracts; they're familiar, common, and sometimes seem overused.

"Love the Lord your God . . . with all your heart."
—Jesus (Mark 12:30)

But these three simple words communicate the most amazing truth in the universe—and they're the most important three words you'll ever tell your child.

God's love isn't a matter of a yellow-faced smile, a surfacy good feeling, or a pithy saying. God's love for us is so miraculous and so incredible and so deep that we can't even understand it without God's help! Paul hinted at this when he wrote to the Ephesians, saying, "I pray that you, being rooted and established in love, may have power, together with all the saints, to grasp how wide and long and high and deep is the love of Christ" (Eph. 3:17–18).

Ultimately one of your most important and critical responsibilities in life is to give your child a sense of *how* God regards him: with infinite, intimate, enduring love. And as your child begins to grasp how deep God's love for him is, he'll naturally respond in kind with his own growing, heartfelt love for God.

the power of feelings

As the soul, mind, and strength sections of this book emphasize, loving God is certainly about much more than feelings. But let's not give feelings a bad rap! The ideas in this section are all about our feelings—our heart. After all, God created emotions as a central component of our lives. He designed our feelings to draw us to him and to respond to him with love and delight. He designed happiness and pleasure and surprise, and he also gave us the capacity for sadness and loneliness and guilt. Our God-given feelings are meant to play a key role in our spiritual growth. So in this section, you'll discover ideas for tapping into those emotions to help your child develop a full sense of God's love for him, respond with feelings of love for God, and understand how God uses our feelings to help us grow closer to him.

You'll also find creative ways to key in on two important emotional components of faith: feelings of *awe* and feelings of *closeness* with God.

Awe. When we stop and consider the reality of God's breathtaking power and the miracles of his creation, we can't help but experience feelings of awe! There are countless opportunities in everyday life to draw your child's attention to God's majesty. For example, you can pause and consider the weather, like thunder or wind or a brilliant rainbow, to take in a sampling of God's astounding power. Or you can emphasize the detail in a tiny leaf's veins, count the spots on a ladybug, or look together at your child's own unique fingerprint to draw your child's thoughts toward the incredible details of God's artistry.

When we really consider who God is and what he's like, we instinctively respond with feelings of awe. Feelings of awe are the precursors of worship, fueling other emotions like longing, joy, love, and devotion to God. As you foster a natural, childlike awe of God, your child will respond with praise and devotion to him.

Closeness. As a new mom, I'd try to ease my young son's fears whenever there were thunderstorms by saying things like, "Look at the brilliant lightning. Isn't God powerful?" or "Listen to those loud crashes. They show us Jesus' awesome power!"

But one day my son told me he didn't want to go to heaven.

"Why?" I asked, in a bit of distress.

In a frightened voice he answered, "Because Jesus is there . . . and he's so . . . so . . . *powerful.*"

I realized right away the mistake I'd made! I'd drawn ample attention to God's power but had neglected another important truth: Not only is God awe-inspiring, but he is also *close.*

God's love is intimate. God isn't out there somewhere raising a ruckus of thunder and scary lightning! He's here with us. He's the Being we were created to love. His love for your child is powerfully devoted, eternally faithful, and familiar. We see in Jesus' life a picture of this love demonstrated in his individual and intimate friendships with Mary, Martha, Peter, John, Mary Magdalene, and others. Like these relationships he had on earth, Jesus can be *your* child's very best friend. With words and stories and trips and games like those outlined in this section, you can cultivate in your child's heart a deep and enduring sense of God's nearness. These feelings of closeness will undergird a lifelong devotion to Jesus.

immeasurable

"God loves you" is a truth that seems so basic we can easily overlook its power. We can lose sight of how profound it is—how experiencing God's love and loving him back changes every aspect of our lives. So what does it mean for *you* to love God with all your heart? It means dropping the familiarity of the phrase and joining your child in the wonder of it all. It means allowing yourself to be awestruck, all over again, at how truly amazing God is. It means letting your heart lead you into worship. It means reveling in the joy and delight of receiving God's love. And it means responding to God with the feelings he gave you—with smiles, happiness, devotion, and committed, lifelong love.

Bernard of Clairvaux once wrote, "You want me to tell you why God is to be loved and how much. I answer, the reason for loving God is God himself; and the measure of love due to Him is immeasurable love." As your love for God shines through, your child will mirror you in engaging his feelings with his faith. For God *deserves* our love. All of it. In fact, more than we can ever give.

color prayers 1

*Use crayons to pray
in a new way.*

experience

supplies:
- paper
- crayons

Gather around the kitchen table with paper and crayons and invite your child to join you in coloring "prayers." Invite her to draw pictures for God—pictures that depict her thoughts and feelings. Encourage her to be as concrete or abstract as she wants. For example, a child might draw a picture of a friend who is sick. Or a child might use colors to depict her feelings (like blue scribbles for sadness or red zigzags for anger). As your child draws, do nothing more than encourage her to express her feelings through her drawings; don't ask her what she's depicting or guide her in what to draw. In fact, the more unclear the object of her drawing appears to you, the better!

connection

Sometimes when we pray, we can't even find the words to express what we feel. But we don't need words. Scripture reassures us in Romans 8:26–27 that God's Spirit not only knows our deepest feelings, but helps us pray when we cannot find the words to express those prayers.

God knows every thought, feeling, and request represented in your child's drawing even if you don't have a *clue* what those scribbles mean. And that's the point here: to foster a sense of intimacy between your child and God, without Mom or Dad included in the communication. This activity affirms for your child that she doesn't need your help to talk to God—God is attentive to your child's own prayers. As your child draws, reassure her of this idea by saying something as simple as, "God knows just what you're feeling and expressing through your drawing. He understands you! It's a prayer just between the two of you."

exploration

You may want to ask your child questions like these:

* What did you think about "praying" without words? Did you like it? Why or why not?
* God knows exactly what you're praying about—he knows each feeling and thought in your heart. How does that make you feel?
* What might be some other fun or unusual ways we can pray to God as a family?

empty inside : 2

Help your child explore feelings of loneliness as you fry up some easy doughnuts together.

experience

Every kid loves doughnuts, and your child will *really* love making his own! But these doughnuts won't only taste good—they'll also serve as an avenue for connecting with your child if you notice he's been feeling lonely or a bit down.

supplies:
- ingredients (see below)
- kitchen tools (including a ¾- to 1½-inch diameter cutter of some type; see ideas below)
- paper towels

connection

The shape of a doughnut represents a common human experience: that feeling of having an emptiness inside. Great theologians such as Blaise Pascal, G. K. Chesterton, and C. S. Lewis wrote about this in the spiritual sense, describing the God-shaped vacuum inside us that can only truly be filled by faith in Christ. But this is also something we deal with on an emotional level. Even joyful followers of Jesus have times of an inner sadness—a sense of loneliness, isolation, or emptiness—that can result from relationship difficulties, life circumstances, or for no apparent reason at all. For kids, this may take the form of crying or feeling afraid to be alone at night; or it may result from not having any friends to play with. On a more serious level, these feelings can result from being bullied, having a dear friend move away, or dealing with a loved one's death.

If your child is dealing with inner sadness, it's imperative that you assure him of God's constant presence. First acknowledge the pain your child is feeling—avoid the temptation to brush over it and simply urge your child to "cheer up." Next, affirm that God knows and understands your child's feelings. It may be helpful to tell your child that even Jesus

30-second doughnuts

ingredients

doughnuts
- canned refrigerated biscuits
- peanut oil

optional toppings
- powdered sugar
- icing
- sprinkles
- cinnamon sugar (1 part cinnamon to 4 parts sugar)

Fill a pot or sauté pan with about 2 inches of peanut oil and preheat on medium-high.

Open up a tube of biscuit dough and separate the biscuits. With your child, use a ¾- to 1½-inch diameter cutter—such as a clean soda bottle top, a tiny biscuit or cookie cutter, an apple corer, a cleaned children's medicine measuring cup, a citrus juice-sipper, a narrow baby bottle top, and so on—to form a hole in the center of each biscuit. Set the biscuits and "holes" on a plate, ready to be fried.

Next, set out paper towels and also ready your toppings. If you'll be making cinnamon sugar or powdered sugar doughnuts, put a big scoop of each in two separate brown paper bags.

Now, only the parent should do this part: Use tongs to set 2 or 3 biscuits in the hot oil and let them fry until one side is golden brown; if your oil is hot enough, this should take just about 15 seconds. Flip the doughnuts to fry for another 15 seconds on the other side; then set them on the paper towel to drain. Repeat this process with all the biscuits. Be sure to fry the "holes" too.

When the doughnuts have drained off any excess hot oil, place them, 1 or 2 at a time, in one of the topping bags, fold over the edges, and invite your child to gently shake the bag to coat the doughnuts. Repeat until they're all done.

Alternately, use icing to frost the doughnuts and doughnut holes; then decorate them with sprinkles.

Eat these tasty doughnuts while they're still warm. Yum!

experienced sadness, such as the time he cried when his friend Lazarus died (John 11:35).

As you make doughnuts together, take time while you cut out the doughnut holes to talk briefly and simply about loneliness. For example, you could say, "Have you ever felt empty inside like this doughnut? I have." Use open-ended questions to draw out anything your child might want to say to express his own feelings. Then, after you've made the doughnuts, have some fun mixing and matching doughnut holes with different types of frosting; try to push some of the doughnut holes back in. (It probably won't work, but it will be fun to try together.) Say something simple like, "God can fill the emptiness we feel inside when we're lonely. Now, this doughnut hole won't fit, but God is a perfect fit and his love can fill us up when we're feeling down."

This doughnut-making activity is just one avenue of addressing loneliness or sadness in your child's life. Allow this experience to be fun—reserve time later on for a more serious heart-to-heart conversation with your child.

exploration
   You may want to ask your child questions like these:

   * Is there anything that's made you feel sad or lonely
     or empty inside lately? Want to talk about it?
   * What's it like to feel lonely?
   * Do you want me to pray for you right now?
     What would you like me to pray about?

3 gobbling up monsters

Make and eat monster cookies to help your child battle her fears.

supplies:
- ingredients (see below)
- kitchen tools

experience

Monster cookies were a childhood favorite of mine. They're monstrous in size and monstrously delicious, filled with all sorts of goodies kids love. Use the recipe below to make monster cookies with your child.

connection

From the bogeyman in the closet to dinosaurs in the backyard, many children deal with irrational fears. These fears may seem silly to us, but they can feel gravely and painfully frightening and real to little ones, especially at bedtime. Use this opportunity to bring these "monsters" into the light. As you make the cookies together, explain why they're called monster cookies: because they're big and have tons of ingredients. Then talk with your child about any childhood fears you had when you were young, particularly any fears of imaginary monsters. Invite your child to tell you about anything she's afraid of and acknowledge the gravity of those fears with words of reassurance, such as, "Yes, I imagine it can feel frightening when you think about that."

my mom's monster cookies

ingredients

- 3 eggs, beaten
- 1 c. packed brown sugar
- 1 c. granulated sugar
- 1 c. chunky peanut butter
- ½ c. butter, softened
- 2 tsp. baking soda
- 1 tsp. vanilla
- 1 tsp. light corn syrup
- 4½ c. quick-cooking rolled oats
- ¾ c. M&Ms
- ¾ c. milk chocolate chips

- Dish of extra sugar (about ½ c.)

Preheat oven to 350 degrees.

In a large bowl, combine eggs, sugars, peanut butter, butter, baking soda, vanilla, and corn syrup. Beat well. Add oats, M&Ms, and chocolate chips, and blend them in thoroughly.

Use an ice cream scoop or a ¼-cup measure to drop globs of the dough onto greased cookie sheets. Remember, you're making *big* cookies! Use the bottom of a glass dipped in sugar to slightly flatten each cookie-dough glob.

Bake for 12–15 minutes, until the edges begin to brown. Allow the cookies to cool a bit before carefully removing them from the baking sheet.

Makes about 2 dozen cookies.

Tell your child directly why she doesn't need to feel afraid of that particular monster. For example, you might say, "I know it feels scary, but you can try to remind yourself that the dinosaur is just imaginary. It isn't real." But then give her the most important reason not to fear: God! Share Isaiah 41:10 with your child and reiterate its most important point: When you feel afraid, God is with you! And God is much more powerful than any imaginary monster or nighttime fear!

When the monster cookies are done baking, name your fears again. Say something like, "Let's pretend your cookie is that imaginary dinosaur . . . and I'll pretend mine is the monster in the closet that I used to be afraid of when I was a child. Let's gobble up those monsters!" Have fun defeating those fears by eating your cookies and laughing together.

exploration

You may want to ask your child questions like these:

* What real or imaginary things make you feel afraid? Why do they frighten you?

* What do you do when you feel afraid? How can we help each other be more brave when we're afraid?

* Is any fear or imaginary monster more powerful than God?

bonus!

The Bedtime Rhyme by Walter Wangerin, Jr. is a charming picture book that tells the tale of a mother reassuring her son in the face of bedtime fears. With fun illustrations and witty rhymes, this book brings home a powerful message: God is in your child's room and, for this reason, she need never fear imaginary monsters again! Read this book together after you gobble up your cookies.

God's love is like these 4

Transform everyday objects into symbols of God's love.

experience

Gather twenty or more items from your home in a large cardboard box. Include a very wide variety of items like:

supplies:
- cardboard box
- twenty household items

* kitchen gadgets (egg beater, funnel, whisk, spatula, kitchen timer, sponge)
* food items (cinnamon stick, marshmallow, orange)
* junk drawer items (rubber band, tape, paper clip, sticky note, calculator)
* clothing (sock, shoe, hat, warm sweater, belt, sunglasses)
* toys (car, baby doll, puzzle piece, picture book, stuffed animal)
* toiletries (cotton ball, tissue, bar of soap, toothbrush)
* miscellaneous (light bulb, battery, key, remote control, cell phone, family picture, figurine)

If your child wants to help, invite him to find and collect five different items from around the house to add to the box.

Once you have your box filled, close the top and sit down next to it with your child. Invite your child to play a simple game with you by turning the objects into symbols that mean something important. To do so, take turns closing your eyes and reaching inside the box. Grab hold of something, pull it out, and then use it to finish this sentence: "God's love is like . . ."

For example, you might say, "God's love is like a battery because it gives me energy," or "God's love is like a timer because God always has time to listen to my prayers." Many of your answers will be silly— and some of your child's answers may not make any sense at all—but that's OK. That's what will make this experience fun!

connection

What better truth to contemplate than the amazing love of God? God's love is rich and full and amazing; God shows his love to us in countless ways. This practice of thinking about God's love in unique ways will give your child a greater sense of how dearly he is treasured by his Creator. And when you're done and you return the items to their proper place in your home, he'll be reminded of God's love for him each time he sees them.

exploration

You may want to ask your child questions like these:

* ❋ Which symbol from the box was your favorite? What did it mean to you?
* ❋ Which object was the toughest to come up with a meaning for? Why?
* ❋ What's one way God showed his love for you today?

God's recycling business 5

Turn "garbage" into something valuable to represent how God uses bad things in our lives for good.

experience

Care for the environment by composting your garbage and teach your child valuable lessons in the process. To create the simplest of compost bins, use a nail to make one or more drainage holes at the bottom of a large bucket. (The holes should be about the diameter of a pencil.) With your child, select a spot for it in your backyard, away from normal eating or playing areas. Set the bucket there and, if you'd like, add a layer of about one to three inches of sand at the bottom.

supplies:
- bucket
- hammer and nails
- sand (optional)
- kitchen scraps (see below)

Explain to your child that composting is a natural process in which organic material (like dead leaves) turns into nutrient-rich soil. As you cook, eat, and dispose of other waste, you'll work as a family to be attentive to which items can go in the compost bucket rather than the garbage can. You can compost things like:

✻ vegetable cuttings and peelings
✻ eggshells (crushed is best)
✻ banana peels and other fruit waste

* leaves and grass clippings
* shredded paper, newspaper, or paper towel (but not too much)
* teabags and coffee grounds

Be sure that you don't put the following in your compost bucket:

* citrus peels (they take a long time to decompose)
* meat or dairy products (they will attract scavenging animals)

Collect materials until your compost bucket is full, allowing a span of several months for the material to turn into nutrient-rich dirt. Every so often, sneak a peek at your compost together and check out the decomposition process at work. It may smell just a tad, but that's OK! In warm weather, the materials will turn into compost over a span of about three to six months. When it does, use the compost with your child as soil for planting bulbs, shrubs, flowers, or vegetables.

connection

It's not often that we look at garbage and see something valuable, but God does. This is one of the most amazing truths of the Christian life: God turns awful, horrible, ugly, smelly, junky, garbage-like experiences and tough circumstances into good. Joseph knew about awful circumstances: He'd been abused (and nearly killed!) by his brothers, sold into slavery, falsely accused, and jailed. But Joseph also knew a powerful truth and told his brothers, "You intended to harm me, but God intended it for good" (Gen. 50:20). The book of Romans also reassures us that "in all things God works for the good of those who love him" (Rom. 8:28). You can use this activity to show your child that every single life experience, even those that feel like pure garbage to us, can be used and transformed by God for the ultimate good. Lead your child to think through the experiences that seem pretty junky and stinky to her and help her begin to imagine how God might be at work turning those circumstances into ultimately good things.

When your garbage begins to truly transform into soil, it will seem like a miracle to your child. The brown, rotting banana peel is no more! It's now just beautiful, rich soil! And it *is* a miracle . . . a tangible, symbolic expression of God's amazing way of working in our lives.

exploration

You may want to ask your child questions like these:

* When have you experienced something bad or upsetting—something that felt like garbage to you?
* Has something that seemed bad in your life ever turned out to be something good? How was God involved?

6 hidden-away hope

*Plant bulbs together to help your child ponder
what it means to hope in Christ.*

supplies:

- flower bulbs
  (such as tulips,
  lilies, irises, etc.)
- gardening
  gloves
- one or more
  hand spades
  or shovels

experience

In the late fall, take your child with you to buy some flower bulbs. Show him the pictures of the flowers these bulbs will become—it's hard to believe that such beauty can come from such plainness! When temperatures have begun to cool (a few weeks of fifty degrees or below at night), bring your child out to help you plant the flower bulbs. (It's best to plant bulbs about six weeks before the soil freezes for winter.) Dig the holes to the proper depth with your child's help; then examine the bulbs together. Look at how unremarkable each bulb appears: just a knotty, flaky, dead-looking, round ball. Then place your bulbs in the holes (root side down), bury them together, and wait for spring!

connection

As you plant the bulbs together, use them to explore the meaning of hope. Talk to your child about how once you've planted the bulbs, the weather will begin to get colder. Soon the soil will freeze, the ground may become covered with snow, and many plants will die. Explain that the bulbs actually *need* to go through the frozen, cold time—it's part of the process that leads to their growth and new life in the spring.

Say something like, "When we believe in Jesus, we have a special hope. We have hope in Jesus' forgiveness, in God's plan, and ultimately we have the hope of going to heaven to be with God someday. This hope is tucked away in our hearts and it lives within us even when we go through hard times. Sometimes our life may feel like winter—we may feel sad, we may feel hopeless, we may even feel frozen. But our hope is still there, hidden away. And God uses even those cold times in life to help us grow."

Use the questions below to talk about hope from your child's perspective. Then, if you aren't too cold, pray together outside, thanking God for giving you both a strong hope that will endure through the difficult winters of life.

And when those flowers bloom months later, you'll remember planting them with your child. On a warm, sunny day, pull your child aside to sit by the flowers for a moment and talk again about hope. Celebrate the beauty of the flowers and recall what you discussed when you first planted the plain, dull bulbs.

exploration

You may want to ask your child questions like these:

* What do you think it means to have hope?
* What do you hope these bulbs will turn into? What do you think they might look like in the spring or summer?
* Have you ever gone through a time that felt like "winter"— a time that was difficult, or painful, or when your heart felt cold or alone? When was that?
* How can a person hold on to hope in Jesus in the middle of a cold time in life?

7 is God crying?

*Watch rain on a window as you consider
what makes God happy and sad.*

supplies:
• none

experience

Next time there's a rainy, dreary day, grab some pillows and create a comfy spot in front of a window where you and your child can quietly watch raindrops trace their way down the glass. Snuggle up and watch the rain fall; listen to the sounds of the raindrops, wind, and thunder. Look together at the water droplets gathering on your window and at puddles forming outside.

connection

Is God crying? Many young children wonder about this when they watch the rain. The apparent teardrops falling from "heaven" can naturally lead to a discussion about God's feelings. If your child doesn't make the observation on her own, observe that the rain looks like tears. Ask your child about what makes her feel sad or makes her cry. Then say something like "What kinds of things do you think make God sad?"

There's a fine line to walk theologically here because God does not have feelings in the same way we experience them. God's character is unchanging and sovereign; he is not subject to emotional turmoil. However, Scripture does make clear that God experiences divine emotion. He rejoices and delights in his creation and he feels love for us. God also feels sadness; he is grieved by sin and its consequences. Jesus wept when Lazarus died and he saw Mary and Martha's deep pain (John 11:35). God was grieved by the repeated idolatry and sinfulness of his people in the Old Testament (Ps. 78:40). And Scripture makes clear that our choices can hurt God; Paul wrote to the Ephesians, "Don't grieve God. Don't break his heart" (Eph. 4:30 MSG).

Talk with your child about human behaviors and tragedies that sadden or grieve God. Then transition to a happier note by talking about things that please God.

exploration

You may want to ask your child questions like these:

* When do you feel sad?
* Do you think God knows what it's like to be sad? Why or why not?
* What kinds of things make God feel really sad?
* What makes God happy?

8 life's ups and downs

*Visit a playground together to teach
your child a valuable lesson about
going through the rough times in life.*

supplies:
• none

experience

Take your child to a favorite playground and spend time playing together. Don't just watch—get right in there and play along! Be sure to push your child on the swings and also to swing together, side by side, seeing who can swing higher. And most essentially, take your child down the slides *with you*, either on your lap or with your arms around each other train-style. After playing together, take time to talk and pray on your way home using the suggestions outlined below.

connection

Nothing feels quite as great as being a child and swinging high up into the air or zipping down a slide. These fun, familiar playground experiences can serve as powerful metaphors for the emotional ups and downs your child is sure to experience in life. As you walk or drive home after playing, use the questions below to explore the emotional highs and lows we all experience. As you talk together, if your child shares any particular heartaches he is facing right now, be certain to stop and pray. Invite your child to join you in prayer with words or in quietness.

As you wrap up your discussion, share the most important point: Just like you went down the slide with your child, God goes with us even during the deepest lows in our lives. Share the words of Joshua 1:9 and Isaiah 43:2–3 with your child as you reassure him that though we may feel discouraged, sad, confused, or frustrated during those times, one thing is certain: God has not abandoned us. He is with us during the times of joy and during the times of hardship.

exploration

You may want to ask your child questions like these:

* What kinds of feelings are like being "up"? What kinds of feelings are like being "down"?
* What experiences have made you feel happy, peaceful, or joyful? What experiences in your life have made you feel down, discouraged, frustrated, or sad?
* Life is full of both ups and downs; in the future, you'll have wonderful experiences and you'll also face tough times. How do you think God will help you get through those different feelings and experiences?
* How does it comfort you to know that God is with you, even when you experience down times in life?

9 made by the master artist

Tour an art museum to help your child discover her inestimable value.

supplies:
• none

experience

Plan a visit to your local art museum with your child. Prepare your child for the museum by looking at some art books together and asking simple questions, such as, "Which picture do you like most? What is beautiful about this painting? If you were an artist, what would you want to create?" Also review some basic rules of museum behavior: no touching the art, no running, no yelling. Finally, get ready by checking the museum's Web site or calling to talk to a curator to find out which pieces of art in the museum are the most famous, the most valuable (monetarily), or are made by the most famous artists.

When you arrive at the museum, use a map to plan what you'll see together and be sure to include the most valuable pieces in your tour. As you look at the art, talk about the pieces again in simple terms, discussing what you like or dislike, which images are your favorite, and so on. When you look at particularly valuable or famous pieces, point out their worth and ask basic questions like, "Why do you think this piece is worth so much money?" or "Why do you think the artist who made this is so famous?" If your museum is able to provide specific financial information, point out the "price tag" of some of the most famous or expensive pieces.

(Be aware ahead of time of how long you want your visit to be. With a younger child who's pre-K or early elementary age, you'll likely want to be there just thirty minutes to one hour.)

connection

The most valuable pieces of art at your museum are likely those created by the most famous artists. In financial terms, the more famous the artist, the more valuable his creation! The *Mona Lisa* is thought to be the most valuable painting on the planet; in fact, it's so valuable that there isn't a price for it because no one can accurately estimate its worth in financial terms. The fact that it was created by da Vinci has a lot to do with its inestimable value. Like pieces by da Vinci, paintings by famous artists such as Renoir, van Gogh, and Picasso are some of the most expensive in the world.

Ask your child, "Who do you think is the most famous and most amazing artist of all time?" After she shares her thoughts, tell her that God is the greatest artist of all time. He created the planet, the stars, the animals, the plants, and each of us. Tell your child, "God, the master artist, made *you*. You are his masterpiece."

Next, talk to her about what this says about her value in this world. She was created, with great care and love, by the supreme artist of the universe! This means that her worth, as a work of the master artist, is incalculable. As your child begins to grasp how awesome and amazing God is, she'll start to understand how special that means *she* is. She is God's handiwork. She is God's creation. The *Mona Lisa* pales in comparison with each human being's value before God!

exploration

You may want to ask your child questions like these:

✶ Of all the pieces of art we saw in the museum, which was your favorite? Why?

* Which of the especially famous and expensive pieces of art did you like? Why?
* Do you often think of yourself as a work of art? Why or why not?
* How special do you think you are to God?
* How does it feel to know you are God's masterpiece? To realize you were made by the greatest artist of all time?

bonus!

Explore this topic further with your child by looking online at images of the world's most expensive paintings. You can find more information and links to images at http://www.renoirgallery.com/most-expensive-paintings.asp and http://en.wikipedia.org/wiki/List_of_most_expensive_paintings.

peace bottle 10

Create wave bottles to explore how
God can bring peace when we feel upset.

experience

Begin with an empty, clean, clear plastic soda bottle and invite your child to help you fill it about one-third to one-half full of water (using the funnel). Assist your child in squeezing just three to four drops of food coloring into the bottle. Next, use the funnel to carefully fill the bottle to the top with mineral oil. Twist the lid on tight and, if you'd like, use a hot glue gun at the base of the lid to seal it.

When the glue is cooled, invite your child to try different things with the bottle, such as:

supplies:
- mineral oil (or other clear oil such as vegetable or peanut)
- water
- food coloring (any color)
- funnel
- clear plastic soda bottle (about 20 oz.) with cap
- hot glue gun (optional)

* holding it horizontally and rocking it from side to side to create waves;
* wildly shaking the bottle, then letting it sit to watch the liquids settle;
* swirling the bottle around to create a funnel shape inside;
* quickly flipping the bottle upside down;
* shaking it up, then counting how long it takes for the liquids to separate again.

The water and oil will always separate and return to their original state: water on the bottom, oil on the top.

connection

Just like grownups, kids' emotions can often feel jumbled up and volatile. One minute your child is happy; the next he's furious, crying, or withdrawn. It's essential that we help our kids learn that the only right way to deal with turbulent emotions is to bring them to God and seek peace in him.

Use the wave bottle to talk about feelings with your child. For example, tell your child about a time you felt angry; shake the bottle as hard as you can and say, "I felt *this* angry!" Or invite your child to talk about a time recently when he felt frustrated; invite him to slosh around the wave bottle to show how he felt inside. Then share with your child the important truth that God created us with feelings and he understands them. Say something like, "If you feel angry, you can talk to God about why you feel that way. Or if you feel sad, you can talk to God about what's got you down."

Next, let the water and oil settle and tell your child about a time when you felt peaceful and calm. Invite your child to share an example of his own. Talk about the peace God gives us and share Isaiah 26:3 with your child: "You, LORD, give true peace to those who depend on you, because they trust you" (NCV). Help your child discover that trusting in God is the key to feeling true peace inside.

exploration

You may want to ask your child questions like these:

* What things or experiences have made you feel really mad lately?
* What's made you feel sad or discouraged lately?
* When have you felt peaceful or calm inside recently? What helps you feel peace inside?

peeled away 11

Eat a healthy snack and show your child that God knows her well, inside and out.

experience

Eat bananas together, carefully peeling the skin back a bit at a time as you eat. Reserve a whole banana to use in a short discussion with your child.

supplies:
• bananas

connection

Everybody sees what's on our outside: our hairstyle, our body type, our facial expressions, our clothing. But God sees what is inside of us. What an awesome, liberating truth!

Use this experience to emphasize to your child that "God knows and deeply loves the *real you.*" In our world, even among the smallest of children, people begin labeling and identifying others based on externals. It can be as simple as, "I like that girl with the curly black hair" to "I want to be his friend because he has the coolest toys." But God doesn't size us up by our appearance or our talents or our abilities or our style or our belongings; God looks into the heart.

Use the unpeeled banana to discuss this idea. Together evaluate its outward appearance. Is it bright yellow? Does it have any brown freckles? Then begin to peel the banana. As you do, make the point that people can only see the outside of a person, but God made us.

He knows us inside and out, and he sees who we really are inside. Share 1 Samuel 16:7, which assures us that "The LORD does not look at the things man looks at. Man looks at the outward appearance, but the LORD looks at the heart."

exploration

You may want to ask your child questions like these:

❋ What are some things people know about you based on your outsides? (Prompt your child to think not just about her physical appearance, but also other externals like clothing style, possessions, or hobbies.)

❋ What are some things people might not know about you if they only looked at your outsides?

❋ How do you feel about the idea that God knows the *real* you—who you are inside?

snuggle up 12

Make a no-sew blanket to help your child discover God's role as his true comforter.

experience

Involve your child, from start to finish, in the process of making a special, snuggly blanket for bedtime. First, take your child to the fabric store with you to select two pieces of fleece fabric. One piece will be the front of the blanket and the other will be the back, so help your child select pieces that are color coordinated.

Purchase the fabric in the dimensions listed. Then, when you get home, follow these steps to help your child create his blanket. (If your child is too young to use sharp scissors with supervision,

supplies:
- 2 pieces of fleece fabric (each 1¾ yards long; 40–54 inches wide)
- scissors
- ruler
- washable (water-soluble) marker
- square piece of paper (about 4 x 4 inches)

do steps 1–5 yourself and lead your child in completing steps 6 and 7.)

1. Lay the pieces of fleece on top of each other with the fuzzy sides facing out. Cut along the edges as needed to make sure they line up well. Also, if your fabric has a selvage edge, cut it off.

2. Place the square piece of paper on one corner of your blanket and trace it with the marker. Do the same on all the corners.

3. Keeping both pieces of fabric together, cut out the square shape traced onto each corner.

4. Use a marker and ruler to draw dots around the edges of the top piece of fleece, approximately one inch apart. (These dots will indicate where you are going to cut your fringes.)

5. Keeping both pieces of fabric together, use the dots as your guide to cut fringes (about four inches deep) all around the edges of the blanket.

6. Now start to tie your blanket together. To do so, tie two corresponding fringe pieces (top and bottom) together in a simple knot. Skip the next fringe; then tie a knot on the next one. Continue to tie knots on every other fringe pair around the entire blanket.

7. Flip your blanket over and, now with the bottom of the blanket facing up, tie the remaining fringe pairs into knots.

Voila! A snuggly, warm, cuddly blanket! Wrap up your child in his blanket and thank him for helping you make it.

connection

When a child is sick, scared, sleepy, sad, or lonely, there's nothing quite as comforting as snuggling up with a favorite blanket or teddy bear. Something about the familiar, soft texture of a comfort object can soothe a child's heart . . . often better than our words or even our hugs.

When your child cuddles up in his new blanket, let him know that God knows all about our feelings and it's no surprise to him that we need comfort at times. Tell your child that the Bible calls God "the Father of compassion and the God of all comfort" (see 2 Cor. 1:3–7), and invite your child to think of God's loving care and comfort each time he snuggles up with this new blanket.

exploration

You may want to ask your child questions like these:

* What do you like about your blanket? Why did you pick these fabrics?
* When do you most like to cuddle up with a blanket? What's fun or special about snuggling up?
* What comforts you when you feel hurt or sad? Words and hugs from people? Cuddling with a blanket or teddy bear? Something else?
* How does God comfort us?

13 soaring hope

Use kite-flying to help your child learn how to best navigate the turbulent winds of human emotion.

supplies:
• a kite

experience

On a moderately windy day (about five to fifteen miles per hour), take your child to an open outdoor area and fly a kite together. Enjoy the challenge of helping the kite take off; show your child how to keep tension in the string. Have fun as you watch your kite soar higher and higher!

connection

Emotions can be like gusty winds. Sadness, anger, and hurt can blow us down and knock us over, making us even more discouraged and frustrated. Happiness, excitement, and surprise can give us an emotional high, a feeling like nothing can go wrong. But it can be tough to navigate life if we let our emotions control us, blowing us this way and that.

The Bible uses a beautiful word picture in Isaiah, saying that "those who hope in the LORD . . . will soar on wings like eagles" (Isa. 40:31). Hope in God is a constant—it doesn't surge or fade like emotions do. It's an underlying current that lifts us up above circumstances and feelings and allows us to soar. And eagles don't soar by furiously beating their wings; they let the current of air lift and carry them. Similarly, when we truly put our hope in God, we allow ourselves to rest in that hope as it lifts us up above the painful feelings and difficult circumstances that come our way.

Depending on your child's age, you may want to stick with the very basic idea here by sharing Isaiah 40:31 and comparing your kite to the soaring eagle in the verse. You could simply talk about what it means to hope in God. But if your child is old enough to be able to recognize the effects feelings have on her life, explore the nuances of this idea further. Use the questions below to help her think about the ways the ups and downs of emotions have impacted her life and behaviors. Then strive to define together what it means to put your hope in God and what it might look like to "soar" like an eagle in real life.

exploration

You may want to ask your child questions like these:

* When have bad or difficult feelings gotten you down or affected you in a negative way? Give examples.
* When have good feelings made you feel "up"? Give some examples.
* What do you think it means to hope in the Lord? How is hope like a feeling? How is it different than a feeling?
* How can we help each other keep a steady hope in God even when negative feelings try to bring us down?

bonus!

Want to try to *make* a kite together? Check out these Web sites for ideas and instructions:

* http://www.skratch-pad.com/kites
* http://www.pbs.org/benfranklin/exp_kite.html
* http://www.howtomakeandflykites.com

14 tic-tac-toe, where will you go?

Play a simple paper game to help your child discover how intimately God knows him.

supplies:
- paper
- pens or pencils

experience

Introduce your young child to the classic paper game tic-tac-toe in which partners take turns drawing *X*s and *O*s on a 3 x 3 grid, attempting to get three in a row. Play several rounds together, helping your child first understand the basics of the game, and second, prompting your child to be attentive to defensive play, blocking you from getting three in a row.

Once your child has a good grasp of the game, play a little tournament together, such as the best three out of five games. As you play with your child, try to match his level of play rather than beating him every time!

With an older child, you could do a more complex paper game such as "squares" (also called "dots and boxes"). You can find directions online at http://en.wikipedia.org/wiki/ Dots_and_boxes.

connection

A key to a young child's understanding of tic-tac-toe is the ability to guess the other player's next move and to try to block him. As you play tic-tac-toe with your child, make playful statements alluding to this aspect of the game, like, "I think I know what you're trying to do!" or "I bet you can't guess what I'm going to do next!" When your child successfully blocks you from connecting your *X*s or *O*s, say something like, "Wow! How did you know I was going to try to do that?"

After you play, talk to your child about how you tried to guess each other's moves and prevent each other from getting three in a row. Say something like, "In the game, we can do a pretty good job at guessing what might happen next, but we can never know for sure. But did you know God really *does* know every single move we're going to make? In fact, he knows every thought you'll have before you think it. He knows every word you'll say before you say it!" You can also share the words of Psalm 139:1–4 with your child.

Pondering God's omniscience causes all of us to marvel, so invite your child to consider God's knowledge with awe. But be sure to move beyond that point to a critical accompanying idea: God's closeness to us. He has intimate knowledge of all we say and do and think—yet he continues to love us deeply. He understands us better than any human friend. In fact, he understands us better than we can understand ourselves!

exploration

You may want to ask your child questions like these:

* ✳ How well did we do at trying to guess and block each other's next moves?
* ✳ Can you guess what I'm thinking right now? Do you think I can guess what you're thinking? Why or why not?
* ✳ God knows every thought you'll ever have. He knows what you're thinking this very instant! How does that make you feel?

15 a twist, a tie . . . a masterpiece!

Use tie-dyeing to help your child understand that God uses all the different circumstances in our lives to form us into the people he wants us to be.

supplies:
- various colors of Rit fabric dye or a tie-dye kit (available at craft stores)
- two or more washed and dried white cotton T-shirts
- rubber gloves
- rubber bands
- several buckets
- long-handled utensils (like serving spoons or barbecue tongs)
- water and other supplies needed to mix the dye (varies; follow instructions on box)
- plastic garbage bags to cover your work surface

experience

Have a groovy time introducing your child to the fine art of tie-dyeing! Get everything ready first by selecting a space to work where it's safe to use dye (which might spill and splatter a bit) and where you have access to water, such as the backyard (by the hose) or the garage. Read the instructions on the dye you've purchased to prepare the dye.

Lay the T-shirts out on a flat surface and show your child how to fold, scrunch, and twist the fabric any way she'd like, "tying" it by tightly wrapping it with rubber bands. By the time you're done, your shirts will look like misshapen, rubber-banded, knobby, floppy, twisted pieces of fabric.

Now begin dyeing by dipping various parts of the shirts in different colors of dye; allow each color to set, and rinse each color as needed per your dye's instructions before moving on to another color. It's best to dye with light colors first and to layer brighter or darker colors on top rather than the other way around. If you are using hot dye baths, be sure to attentively supervise and help your child.

When you're completely done dyeing the shirts, rinse them in cool water (if required) then carefully remove the rubber bands and untwist the fabric. Lay your T-shirts out flat, side-by-side, and *ooh* and *ah* together at your amazing designs.

connection

Tie-dyeing can serve as a powerful metaphor for an essential spiritual truth: We can trust in our sovereign, all-knowing God. In life, every event and circumstance and twist and turn affects us. And whether we realize it or not, God has a purpose for all of it: to form and shape us into the person he desires us to become. We can always trust in his omniscience and sovereignty, knowing that he sees the "final product" even when we can't.

As you tie-dye with your child, you really have no idea how the final shirts will turn out. But you'll see together, hands-on, how each twist and knot and fold and tie ultimately contribute to a surprisingly beautiful, cool design. Random scrunches here and there turn out to be essential in creating a one-of-a-kind piece of art.

Help your child make this connection by asking her questions as you twist, knot, tie, and dye your T-shirts. Say, "What do you think tying it this way might do to my shirt?" and "How do you imagine the final masterpiece will turn out?" As you sit and wait for your fabrics to dye, explain the spiritual symbolism of the project in age-appropriate terms. Say something like, "Sometimes our lives can feel like this. Things can happen that feel like twists and turns and knots. We may feel like saying, 'God, I don't understand what's going on.' But God has a plan in mind for us that we can't see. God has a perfect design for our lives! We can always trust in him." You might also want to read and talk about Romans 8:28.

When you untwist and untie your shirts, effusively express amazement at the final designs and reaffirm that God is always at work in your child's life, shaping and forming her into the person God desires her to become.

exploration

You may want to ask your child questions like these:

* Are you surprised by how our shirts turned out? What did you do to your shirt to get this final design?
* When has God used an event in your life to change you or form you? How did it change you?
* How does it make you feel to know that God can use everything in your life for his good purpose and perfect plan?
* How can we help each other trust in God's plan for our lives?

bonus!

Want to try your hand at traditional tie-dye designs? Check out the ideas on web sites like http://www.ritdye.com/Tie-Dye+Patterns.17.lasso or http://familycrafts.about.com/cs/tiedye/a/041601a_4.htm.

the ultimate fort 16

*Create an indoor fort to explore
how God is our shelter.*

experience

Hunker down for some fun by making an indoor fort with your child. Arrange kitchen chairs, couches, plastic crates, or any other indoor materials that can serve as walls. Drape blankets and sheets over top to completely cover the structure. Tuck in the edges at the bottom to make the walls and roof taut. Do some interior decorating by putting pillows, blankets, and other comforts like a favorite stuffed animal, books, and flashlights inside. Then let your imaginations take over!

supplies:
- blankets and bed sheets
- pillows
- furniture (like chairs, couches)
- flashlights (optional)

Hide out in your fort together and lead your child in various pretend scenarios such as a wild rainstorm raging outside the fort. Imagine that you hear wind and thunder as you huddle up inside the protection of your fort. Or pretend you hear a bear outside your fort; playact peeking out the door, then hurrying back inside once you see the scary animal. Or imagine that you live in the pioneer days and this fort is your only protection during a blizzard. In every imaginary scenario, emphasize that the fort is a place of safety.

connection

Life can be frightening, tiring, pressure filled, and dangerous—and your kids aren't immune to this reality. Our culture is ready with "answers" to this problem. For adults, the message is to escape through overwork, sports, dream vacations, shopping sprees, partying, or worse. But our culture also offers false answers to our kids, like escaping through video games and television, the lure of buying the next new toy, or the message that loving oneself is the true source of contentment. Though some of these things do offer temporary respite from struggles and stress, they won't truly weather the storm. Only God is a true and trustworthy shelter for us.

In the evening after you've played in your fort, lead your child through a different imagination exercise: a prayer experience focused on God. Close your eyes together and prompt your child to imagine the tough things he faces in the world. Then share the idea from Scripture that God is your child's shelter—he can run to God for protection and safety and true security. If you'd like, share Psalm 91:1–2 to aid his imagination-prayer. You can even lift your arms above your heads to form a shelter over yourselves as you pray this way. Say something like, "Imagine the strongest, toughest, safest fort ever. Nothing can get through its walls. And though outside there might be danger, inside it is warm and safe and peaceful and comforting. That's what God is like. Imagine going into that fort of God's protection and shelter."

Instead of ending with the traditional "amen," let your child continue to imagine until he drifts off into sleep (or starts chatting again).

exploration

You may want to ask your child questions like these:

* Sometimes life is tough and we want to run and hide. Are there things going on in your life right now that make you feel that way?
* How has God been like a fort or shelter for you? How has he kept you safe or provided comfort for you?

worm hunt **17**

Amaze your child as she considers God's intricate knowledge of every creature on the planet—even worms!

experience

After (or during) a thorough rain, venture outside with your child to hunt for worms. You shouldn't have to look too hard—you'll likely find several stranded on sidewalks, driveways, or in garden puddles. (Try to steer your child toward *living* worms.) If she's gutsy, encourage your child to pick up a worm and look at it, noting its size, shape, and color. Laugh together as the worms tickle your hands. Then put the creatures back down in a worm-friendly area, like a garden or your front lawn. (If your child is enjoying the worm hunt, give her an extra challenge: "rescuing" the worms from the driveway or sidewalk and delivering them all to the flowerbed.)

As you look at the worms together, see if your child is surprised by the number of worms she's found. Invite her to guess how many worms live in your yard.

supplies:
- rubber boots
- umbrellas

connection

Scientists estimate that in an average yard, there are as few as five to as many as twenty-five or more earthworms *per cubic foot* of topsoil. Talk to your kids about how there are hundreds or even thousands of worms in your yard, living and eating below the surface. Other than during rainstorms, you usually don't see them—but God does.

God knows about and cares for every single creature he created, even those that are hidden from our sight. God knows what each and every one of us is up to, from a mighty elephant to a human child to an earthworm. God knows *everything*. Share Luke 12:6–7 with your child, emphasizing God's knowledge of intricate details and his care for the life of a small bird. You may also want to talk about Matthew 6:25–29, a passage that emphasizes God's care not just for birds but also for flowers.

As you consider together how truly awesome and incomprehensible God's knowledge is, foster in your child feelings of awe and wonder at God's greatness and goodness. Help her to emotionally connect with the truth that God loves and cares for her—and knows every intricate detail about her life.

exploration
You may want to ask your child questions like these:

* Imagine it was your job to keep track of all the worms in our yard and to know everything about each one of them. Could you do it? Would you *want* that job? Why or why not?
* Now think about God's "job": knowing about and caring for every single creature on this entire planet. How do you feel when you think about how God is able to know, keep track of, and care for *everything* on earth?
* What are some ways God cares for us?

*Play hide-and-seek to give your child a
sense of God as his "hiding place" in life.*

experience

Play several rounds of the old-fashioned game
hide-and-seek. Simply select one player to be "It"
while the other players hide. After a set time (such
as a slow count to twenty), "It" can search for the
other players. When "It" finds another player, that
person becomes "It" in the next round.

supplies:
• none

Be sure to set a few ground rules ahead of time, identifying the
boundary within which players can hide and specifying any unsafe
out-of-bounds areas where kids should not hide.

connection

There's no better hiding place in life than God! In Psalm 31:19–20,
David says God bestows his goodness on those who take refuge in
him, writing, "In the shelter of your presence you hide them . . . in your
dwelling you keep them safe." David also praised God, saying, "You
are my hiding place; you will protect me from trouble and surround
me with songs of deliverance" (Ps. 32:7). These verses use the Hebrew
words *sathar* (verb) and *sethar* (noun), which communicate the idea
of hiding or of making oneself absent. In other words, when God is

our hiding place, it doesn't mean we are hiding *from* something, but rather that we are making ourselves absent from everything and everyone else so we can be with God.

As your child hides during this game, he'll experience quietness and time alone. He probably won't be thinking a lick about God, but his experience of alone "hiding time" during the game is something you can draw on afterward.

When the game is done and you're sitting down together, share Psalm 32:7 with your child and ask him simply, "Did you know God is our hiding place? What do you think that means?" After affirming your child's responses, invite him to recall what it was like to be hiding and alone during the game. Communicate that God wants to spend time with us like that—just him and us, alone, close, in quietness. Then let your child know God loves him so much that he can have time alone with God and have hidden-away, heart-to-heart conversations. Tell your child about your own habit of spending time alone with God.

exploration

You may want to ask your child questions like these:

✳ Which was the best hiding spot in this game? Why?
✳ Which did you like better: hiding or seeking? Why?
✳ What did you think about when you were hiding? Did you enjoy being quiet and alone? Why?
✳ How is God like a hiding place?

you won't see *that* at the zoo!

19

Take a visual tour of unusual, endangered, or simply outrageous creatures; then sit in awe of God's creative, artistic nature.

experience

Sit down with your child in front of the computer and prepare to be intrigued and amazed as you visit www.arkive.org and view some of the videos there. Arkive is a project funded by various nonprofit organizations and donors that seeks to capture video images and still photographs of all the species of life on earth! Begin by perusing the "Threatened Species" section, or type in one of your child's favorite animals in the search field, select Video, then hit Go. (You can enter very basic words like *bird, monkey, beetle,* or *fish.*) Have fun looking at all sorts of videos together. Parental warning: Be sure to read the video descriptions before pressing Play because, as is the case with most nature footage, some videos do contain images of mating or of predators killing prey.

supplies:
• computer with Internet connection

connection

As you tour www.arkive.org, keep the focus from beginning to end on God as the designer and creator of all these unique and amazing creatures. As you view various videos, talk with your child about what you see, using some of the questions below. God didn't just zap this world into being; he designed thousands of species with unique colors, sounds, feathers, shells, faces, abilities, and instincts. The variety, the artistry, and the beauty of God's creation are overwhelming when we really take the time to look at it! The idea here is to help your child move beyond an intellectual knowledge that God created the world to an inner sense of true awe of God. As you sit together, you may even want to explain the meaning of the word *awe*, helping your child see what it really means to say "God is awesome." Express your own feelings of awe before God as you look at the animals he's made by addressing him aloud during your time together. You could spontaneously say things to God that your child will understand like, "God, it looks like you painted that fish with a paintbrush! You are such an artist!" or "God, it is so wonderful to see all the animals you've made. Each one is a miracle. You amaze me, God."

exploration

You may want to ask your child questions like these:

* What is amazing about this creature?
* What is unique about this creature?
* What's surprising about this creature?
* What do these creatures show us about God and what he is like?
* What do you feel about God after seeing all these creatures he made?

your inner compass

20

*Watch an arrow formation of migrating
birds and consider our own God-given
sense of instinct: the conscience.*

experience

In spring or autumn, keep your ears open for
the telltale honking of geese and your eyes peeled
for the amazing arrow formation of ducks in
the sky . . . It's migration time! Draw your child's
attention to the birds taking their annual journey
south for the winter and back north for the
summertime. If you have a bird-watching manual,
show your child the maps of various bird routes; if
you can, look up the specific migration routes for the type of birds
you've just seen overhead.

supplies:
- binoculars
(optional)
- bird-watching
manual with
migration maps
(optional)

Explain the basics of migration and the mysterious, awe-inspiring
instinct God has given to birds: the ability to sense when it's time to fly
south and exactly where to go, even over hundreds or thousands of
miles! Without maps, without directions, without a compass, without
road signs, these birds know right where to go. How? They just *know.*

connection

Many of us wish we had the inner sense of direction birds have—
it would save us a lot of time on family road trips! But the great

news you can share with your child is that God *has* made us with an amazing instinct: It's the God-given ability to know right from wrong. It's called our conscience, and we can see its existence even in the youngest of toddlers who can't hide a guilty expression when they know they've broken the rules.

Guilt is an emotion that's tough for us to deal with, just as it was for Adam and Eve. Like the first humans, we often hide when we feel guilty. We let shame or discouragement overtake us. We lie or act sneakily to try to cover up what we've done wrong. But the feeling of guilt that pops up when we sin is part of our conscience— our inner compass. It may feel awful, but it's actually an amazing gift from God that helps us sense when we've done wrong. Let your child know that instead of hiding or being sneaky when he feels guilty, he can view guilt as an "instinct" telling him he needs to face what he's done and ask God's forgiveness.

Help your child understand that guilt is a part of life for everyone, no matter the age, and share with him an example of a time you did something you felt guilty about when you were a child. Explain that even great heroes of the Bible felt guilty when they sinned! You may want to share Psalms 38:4 and 51:3 to show your child how David felt the same heavy feelings of guilt he may experience. But then share the proper response to guilt that David models for us: "But I confess my sins; I am deeply sorry for what I have done" (Ps. 38:18 NLT). Thank God together for the inner sense of direction he's given you both.

exploration

You may want to ask your child questions like these:

* ✳ How do you think birds know where to go?
* ✳ Did God make you with any instincts? If so, what are they?
* ✳ When have you felt like something was right or wrong?
* ✳ How can we respond to feelings of guilt?

yummy family portrait **21**

Design and bake a dough family to help your child understand the love and care with which God formed her.

experience

Drawing family pictures and creating models of family members out of play dough is fun, but have you ever made an *edible* portrait of your family? Use the easy dough recipe below to make a bread version of each family member's face. Have a great time being creative and silly together!

supplies:
- ingredients (see below)
- kitchen tools

connection

As you create your silly dough portraits of each member of your family, both you and your child will naturally take great care to make things just right. This process of forming dough-people can give your child just a glimpse of what it means to believe God made each of us. Genesis 2:7 tells us God formed the first man out of the dust of the earth; but God's careful attention to how each human being is made didn't stop with Adam.

Use this experience to show your child that God designed and miraculously formed each one of us. In fact, God placed each freckle on your child's nose, chose the specific color of your child's hair, and determined the exact size of her feet. Nothing about your child

funny-shaped dough

ingredients

- 1 c. whole wheat flour
- 2½ c. white flour
- 1 packet fast-acting yeast (equivalent to 2¼ tsp.)
- 1 tsp. brown sugar
- 1 tsp. salt
- 1½ tbsp. butter, softened
- 1½ c. warm water
- 1 egg, separated
- (optional: chocolate chips)

Mix the dry ingredients together. Cut the butter into pieces and invite your child to pinch and rub it into the dry mix until it's totally blended in.

Pour in the warm water and stir it in. When it's too sticky to stir, use flour-coated hands to begin to knead the dough in the bowl (or turn it out onto a floured surface). To knead it, simply fold it on top of itself, then push it down; make a quarter turn, then fold it over and push it down again. Encourage your child to use the palm or heel of her hand when she kneads. Continue kneading, taking turns with your child, for 6–7 minutes.

Form the dough into a large ball and cover it with a damp towel.

Coat a baking sheet with nonstick spray. Then pinch off chunks of the dough and form them into balls. (Keep the remaining dough covered so it doesn't dry out.)

Together, form medium-sized balls to be faces, flattening them down on the cookie sheet. Form small balls to be eyes and ears; roll "worms" to be smiles, hair, eyebrows, and glasses. Use a garlic press (or Play-doh press) to create thinner pieces of hair. You can also press chocolate chips into the dough to create eyeballs or freckles. Push the pieces of dough gently onto the faces; work quickly before the surface of the dough begins to dry out.

Cover the dough faces with plastic wrap and set the baking sheet in a warm, draft-free place to let it rise for 45 minutes to 1 hour.

Preheat your oven to 425 degrees and put a shallow dish of hot water in the oven to keep the air moist.

When the dough has fully risen (about double in size), use a pastry brush to coat the top of each face with egg white. Then stick them in the oven to bake for 20–25 minutes.

Smaller pieces, like thin strands of "hair," can burn, so check on the dough as it bakes and cover smaller pieces with foil if needed once they've browned.

Serve the faces warm with butter and jam.

(even apparent "flaws") is an accident; God purposefully and lovingly made your child just as she is. Share Psalm 119:73 with your child, which says, "Your hands made me and formed me." Or share Psalm 139:13–15, which says, "Oh yes, you shaped me first inside, then out; you formed me in my mother's womb. . . .You know me inside and out, you know every bone in my body; you know exactly how I was made, bit by bit" (MSG).

Ultimately the goal here is to help your child get a sense of God's great love for her. God knows and cares about every detail of your child and her life. She is special and precious to God! Take an opportunity as you bake together to directly share affirming words with your child, speaking truth about God's deep and enduring love for her.

exploration

You may want to ask your child questions like these:

* Which details about each person in our family are most important to include in our dough portraits?
* How does it feel to know God formed you, paying attention to every single detail about every single aspect of who you are?
* What details did God include when he formed you? How did he make your appearance? (Describe yourself.)
* What did God make you like on the inside? What are your interests and your personality?

bonus!

When the dough portraits rise, they'll start looking pretty funny. Grab a camera and take some silly pictures during the baking and eating process.

Along with our heart (emotions), we are called to love God with all our *soul*—with our whole spiritual being. This soul-love is the engine at the core of spiritual growth; it's a love and devotion to God that drives us to seek after him with determined focus, striving to know him deeply and love him more and more. But soul-love is more than a feeling; it's expressed in our practical efforts to abide in Christ, to live as branches intimately connected to the vine (John 15:5). We show our soul-love for God—and grow in our soul-love for God—through spiritual practices like prayer, meditation, worship, celebration, and others.

"Love the Lord
your God . . .
with all your soul."
—Jesus (Mark 12:30)

Surprisingly, kids are often better able to love God with their souls than us grown-ups. They're more attuned to the wonder of God's world. They're ready and eager to believe in angels and miracles, to whisper to God's invisible presence in their bedroom, to listen eagerly to God's quiet voice. Unlike us adults who are weighed down with responsibilities, children approach God with freedom, ease, and delight. We could learn a thing or two about soul-love from our children!

how God grows us

We parents pay close attention to our kids' physical growth and developmental milestones, but we often don't focus nearly enough on their spiritual formation. I'm not talking about Bible knowledge here (we'll get to that in the next section)—I'm talking about the intimacy they experience with God in their soul. Nurturing soul-love for God in our kids begins with proactively helping them sense God's close presence and connect intimately with him. We can do this by zeroing in on a few key spiritual disciplines.

Prayer. Mealtime and bedtime prayers are a powerful way to help children develop the habit of talking with God. But we must also help our kids learn that they can talk to God at *any* time. We can assure them that God listens, he cares, and he understands. We can help our children discover that just like a human friendship, our relationship with God is deepened as we spend time "getting to know each other" through prayer.

Meditation and Contemplation. Kids are naturals at meditation compared to us cynical and harried adults. For children, this spiritual discipline is best captured in moments of quiet, wide-eyed wonder. The terms *meditation* and *contemplation* can be intimidating; a good way to think of this discipline with children is simply to call it "being still with God" or "listening prayer." The goal here is to help your child experience times of inner quietness and peace (even if the moments are short-lived!). Kids won't practice meditation in the same way as adults—but that's OK! Stamina is not the issue here. Instead the focus should be on fostering comfort with times of quietness and a readiness to wonder at God's awesomeness.

Worship and Celebration. Children love to laugh, smile, and have fun. One of the most significant truths you can pass along to your child is that God is to be *enjoyed*! We do our kids a tremendous disservice if we give them the idea that God-stuff is boring and serious. We don't serve a dour God. We know and love a God who delights in us and wants us to delight in him! You can turn almost any happy moment into a time of worship and celebration by drawing your child's attention to God. It can be as simple as saying, "Thank you, God, for the fun we're having together right now!"

Other "Grown-Up" Spiritual Disciplines. Prayer, times of wonder (meditation), and worship all seem to come naturally to kids. In addition to these essentials, you can also expose your child to practices that may feel new and different to her, but will be powerful spiritual growth tools for her as she grows and matures. This section includes ideas for creative, kid-friendly ways to introduce your child to *confession* (recounting personal sins and asking God for forgiveness), *examen* (taking a close look at one's way of living and inviting God to help one grow and change), and *fasting* (giving up a habit to focus on hunger for God).

God at work

Your role in this endeavor is to love God with all *your* soul and to model for your child habits of intimacy with God that inspire her to seek after the same thing. And as you use these fun, creative experiences to help your child encounter God in this way, God himself will draw her soul to him (John 6:44). As you nurture your child's spiritual formation, you can trust in God's power at work within her (Eph. 3:16–21), tugging her soul in his direction, speaking to her, forming her, guiding her, and connecting with her. "God can do anything, you know—far more than you could ever imagine or guess or request in your wildest dreams! He does it not by pushing us around but by working within us, his Spirit deeply and gently within us" (Eph. 3:20–21 MSG).

22 a to z thanks

*Use a simple alphabet game to
thank God with your child.*

supplies:
• none

experience

Whether your child is just beginning to master his ABC's or is an expert reader, this game presents both a fun challenge and a meaningful time of praise! The game is simple: Take turns thanking God for various things based on letters of the alphabet. There are two basic ways to play it:

(1) With your child, take turns going through the alphabet. For example, you'd go first with the letter A and you might say something like, "God, thank you for *apples.*" Your child goes next and he might say, "God, thank you for my snuggly *bed.*" Repeat this pattern all the way to Z . . . and be ready to come up with some silly thanksgivings for J, Q, X, Y, and Z!

(2) Take turns randomly naming letters for each other. For example, you might say "N" to your child. Your child thinks of something he is thankful for, then responds, "God, thank you for my *nightlight.*" Your child then challenges you with the letter "J" and you respond by saying, "Thank you, God, for *jokes*—it's fun to laugh together!"

connection

Even if it feels like just a silly game, you and your child are actually practicing the spiritual discipline of celebration together. Your time of thanking God is music to his ears—and repeating this game is a great way to form a habit of giving thanks in your child's heart.

After you play, talk a bit more with your child about deeper things you're thankful for, like your relationship with Jesus, your marriage to your spouse, or the privilege of being a parent. Invite your child to also share some meaningful things he is thankful for. If you'd like, read Psalm 30:12 and talk about how we can give thanks to God forever—throughout our lifetime here on earth and when we live with God in heaven.

exploration

You may want to ask your child questions like these:

* ✳ Which letter was the hardest? Which was the easiest?
* ✳ What other things are you most thankful for?
* ✳ Why do you think it's important to say thanks to God?

bonus!

A fun variation of this game is to use Scrabble tiles. Place the tiles face down and take turns drawing a tile and saying thanks based on the letter you drew.

23 bird-watching and God-listening

Go bird-watching with your child and contemplate God's presence together.

supplies:
- binoculars
- outdoor clothing
- bird-watching books (optional)

experience

Take a trip to a local wooded park and set aside about thirty minutes for outdoor exploration and bird-watching. Begin by using bird-watching books to show your child pictures of some of the most common birds in your area. Then explain the basic idea: You'll go on a slow walk, as quietly as you can, listening for the sounds of birds (or other forest noises) and looking for birds in the trees. Remind her that birds will be frightened by your noises, so all talking should be in a hushed whisper.

Go on your bird-watching adventure together. Then sit down and talk about the various animals you saw and noises you heard. Create a list of the birds your child saw (or *thinks* she saw).

connection

Spending "quiet" time in nature is one of the most powerful ways for children to begin the Christian practice of contemplation or meditation. They're simply taking time to quiet their hearts, calm their thoughts, and observe God's world. You may want to emphasize this at the beginning of your bird-watching walk, saying something like, "God made this awesome forest—and he's in the forest with us! As we look and listen for birds, let's also look for things and listen for sounds that remind us of God."

When you debrief together after your walk, lead your child in exploring how she feels after spending time in (relative) quietness. Read Psalm 46:10: "Be still and know that I am God." Then prompt your child to share ways she sensed God's presence or observed things that reminded her of God and his truths.

exploration

You may want to ask your child questions like these:

* What creatures did you see? What sounds did you hear?
* What do you feel like now after spending quiet time in nature? Refreshed? Peaceful? Explain.
* What did this walk show you about God?

bonus!

The National Wildlife Federation has a great Web site full of ideas for outdoor nature experiences for young kids. You can find it at www.greenhour.com.

24 breathe in, breathe out

Introduce your child to a meditative prayer practice that's perfect for bedtime.

supplies:
• none

experience

As you tuck your child into bed at night, invite him to pray with you in a unique way called "breath prayer." Breath prayer is a pattern of silently praying a simple phrase as you inhale, then silently praying a second phrase as you exhale. Use a basic two-phrase prayer with your child, such as, "Thank you, God, for loving me." Lie down by your child and say something like, "Let's quietly and slowly repeat a prayer to God in our minds as we begin to relax and fall asleep." Try to match your pattern of inhaling and exhaling with your child's. Then say the prayer slowly aloud (while your child *thinks* it) about ten times, pacing yourself by your child's breathing rhythm. After a bit, stop saying the prayer and just breathe in and out together for a while. When you're ready to leave the room, invite your child to try to keep praying silently as he falls asleep.

connection

Have you ever felt guilt-ridden about nodding off to sleep during your nighttime prayers? I used to berate myself too, until I learned about this ancient method that aims to form a rhythm of prayer in our hearts that's as regular, constant, and unconscious as breathing. What better way to fall asleep than to have one's last thoughts each night calmly focused on God?

This approach boils prayer down to its most basic element: connection with God. It doesn't include requests or elaborate praises. In fact, it doesn't include much vocabulary at all! But it fosters a sense of connection with God that can sometimes get lost when we're too focused on running through a mental checklist of requests.

Consider creating original breath prayers with your child; as you inhale, address God, and as you exhale, express a praise or a request (for example, "Loving Jesus, help me love others" or "Creator of the world, I worship you"). Or teach your child a traditional breath prayer embraced by Christians in many liturgical traditions called the Jesus Prayer. Based on Luke 18:13 and 39, the Jesus Prayer is: "Lord Jesus Christ, Son of God, have mercy on me, a sinner."

exploration

You may want to ask your child questions like these:

✳ How is praying like breathing? How is it different?
✳ How does praying a breath prayer make you feel?

25 bright as new

Clean tarnished pennies to help your child understand that God "cleans" us when we confess our sins and accept his forgiveness.

supplies:
- several tarnished pennies
- a bottle of hot sauce
- paper towels

experience

Look at some tarnished pennies with your child. Point out how the pennies look dirtied or discolored. Then lead your child in shaking some hot sauce onto one side of each penny. You'll want about ten drops of hot sauce per penny.

Let the hot sauce sit on the coins for five to ten minutes while your child plays with something else. Then, when time's up, have your child use paper towels to wipe the pennies clean and "polish" them a bit. They'll look shiny and new!

Invite your child to flip over the pennies and compare the clean sides with the dirty sides. Ask your child what she thinks about the difference.

connection

As you look at the tarnished sides of the pennies, talk with your child about how we're like the pennies—we sin every day, and that sin dirties our hearts. Then explain that our hearts can be cleaned by Jesus! Tell her that an important part of having a friendship with God is confessing our sins and asking for forgiveness when we do things wrong. If your child doesn't know what confession means, explain that it's simply talking with God and telling him what you did wrong.

Then have your child look at the shiny sides of the pennies. Say something like, "Just like this hot sauce cleaned the pennies, when God forgives us, he washes us clean. God helps us start over, bright and clean, shiny and new! Isn't that awesome?" You may want to read Psalm 51:1–2 and 7 with your child to help her understand what confession looks like. First John 1:9 is another powerful verse to share to reassure your child of God's forgiveness.

Lead your child in putting hot sauce on the remaining tarnished sides of the pennies. As the hot sauce sits on the pennies for about five to ten more minutes, encourage your child to think about her actions and thoughts over the past few days and silently confess any sins to God. After some quietness, pray aloud, saying something like, "God, we do wrong things and we know that they dirty our hearts. Please forgive us for these things. Please clean our hearts. We accept your forgiveness. Thank you for giving us a new start! Amen."

Polish the pennies together, celebrating God's awesome forgiveness.

exploration

You may want to ask your child questions like these:

* What are some of the wrong things we do that dirty our hearts?
* How do these sins hurt our relationship with God?
* How does it feel to talk to God about wrong things you've done?
* How does it feel to know God forgives you?

26 connected

Magnetize nails and paperclips to discover how being connected to Jesus changes us.

supplies:
- 1 or more strong magnets (a bar or ring magnet is preferred)
- 1 or more iron nails
- 15 or more metal paperclips
- a few other metal objects like coins and pieces of jewelry

experience

Enjoy some magnet play with your child by trying these experiments:

1. See what your magnet can pick up. Nails? Paperclips? Coins? Jewelry? Now see what a plain old nail or paperclip can pick up just by touching it. (The answer? Nothing.)

2. Make a magnetized paperclip chain. As he holds the magnet up high, have your child gently connect one paperclip to your magnet. Prompt him to then gently touch another paperclip to the one already hanging; it should attach. Continue to carefully add paperclips to the magnet, seeing how long a chain you can create. Next separate the very top clip from the magnet to see what happens. (All the paperclips will fall down.)

3. Turn a nail or paperclip into a magnet. If you've got a bar magnet, have your child stroke the paperclip or nail *in the same direction* along one half (one pole) of the bar a hundred or more times. If you have a ring magnet, have your child rub the paperclip or nail around the ring in a hundred circles in the same direction.

Your nail or clip should now be a temporary magnet. Attempt to pick up other nails and paperclips together. (Be careful not to flip over or turn the nail or paperclip over during the magnetization process and don't drop or strike your new magnet.)

connection

We can learn a lot from magnetization. In the first experiment, it quickly becomes obvious that only the magnet has the power to attract and pick up objects; the nails and paperclips are powerless. Invite your child to imagine that the magnet is God—only God is all powerful, and we are not.

In the second experiment, the paperclips become temporary magnets as the power of the true magnet flows through them. What a picture of the essence of Christian spirituality! Talk about this experiment and say something like, "Just as the paperclips acted like magnets, when we are connected to God, we become more like him." Invite your child to share ideas about *how* people can be connected with God as well as ways people can become godly.

In the last experiment, the same point is made even more clear. With every stroke on the magnet, your nail or paperclip becomes even more powerfully magnetized. Similarly, the more time we spend in contact with God, the more like him we become.

There are many ways we can be connected with God, but with your child be sure to zero in on spiritual growth practices he can do, such as talking to God (prayer), singing to God (worship), learning Bible stories (listening to Scripture), and learning Bible verses and thinking about them (memorization and meditation). Help your child to see that these ways of being connected to God actually change him in amazing ways.

exploration

You may want to ask your child questions like these:

* What do you think about the way your nail (or paperclip) changed? Were you surprised? Why or why not?
* What are some ways we can "connect" with God?
* How do you think God may be changing you to be more like him?

defensive moves : **27**

Use a game of checkers to help your child think about how to spiritually defend herself.

experience

Play a rowdy game of checkers with your child. Or, if your child is old enough (and you're smart enough!), play chess together instead. As you play, make good use of the words *attack* (as in,

supplies:
- a checkers (or chess) game

"My red checkers are on the attack! We're gonna get you!") and *defend* (as in, "Good job defending your guy! Now I can't jump him."). Do your best to keep the game close, but in the end, be sure to let your child win . . . at least this time!

connection

In both checkers and chess, at least 50 percent of the game is about defending one's own game pieces from attack. If a player is oblivious to the defensive aspect of a game, she's certain to lose. You can use a game like this to introduce your child, in an age-appropriate manner, to spiritual warfare.

With young kids, I don't recommend talking about things like demons or phrases like "spiritual warfare" because it can feel terribly scary and could become the fodder for many nightmares. But you can talk about things like sin, fear, and temptation. For example, you could explain what temptation is, and then you could say something like, "Satan doesn't want us to please God, and one way he tries to get us to sin is with temptation." Share some basic scenarios in which you experience temptation and invite your child to think of ways she feels tempted to sin.

Then frame that type of temptation in terms of checkers, saying, "When Satan tries to attack us with a temptation, we can defend ourselves!" Share Ephesians 6:10–11 and also James 4:7 with your child and talk together about what these passages mean. Share some good "defensive moves" Christians can make: awareness, prayer, resistance, asking others for support, relying on God's strength, and confessing sins.

With an older child, you can talk a bit more openly about spiritual warfare. Read Ephesians 6:10–18 together and talk more frankly about how life can be like a battle and how our Enemy tries to attack us.

Whatever your child's age, firmly reassure your child at the end of the conversation that ultimately we need not fear the Enemy because of how powerful and awesome God is. Pray together and address any fears, temptations, or other areas of need your child has mentioned during your discussion.

exploration

You may want to ask your child questions like these:

* ✳ How important is it to defend your guys in checkers (or chess)? Could someone win if they didn't try to defend their guys? Why or why not?
* ✳ In a spiritual sense, what are some things we need to defend ourselves against?
* ✳ What things or situations make you feel tempted to sin?
* ✳ How can we defend ourselves against temptation (or fear)?

destination: God's ear **28**

*Fly paper airplanes together to help
your child discover that his prayers
always reach their destination.*

experience

Teach your child how to fold paper airplanes
(see the instructions below). Once you've made
several airplanes, practice flying them around the
house. After having some fun races and contests

supplies:
• paper

(like seeing whose plane flies the highest, farthest, or fastest), pretend
your "jets" have to land at a specific destination (the dining room table,
for instance). Play together, and try to fly your jets so they'll all land in
the area you've identified. Laugh with your child when your planes
don't make it, and celebrate together when they do.

connection

As you try to fly your airplanes to a specific landing spot, more than
likely you'll discover that many of them have missed the hoped-for
destination. After the activity, talk with your child about prayer. Hold
up one of the airplanes and say something like, "Imagine this is a
prayer. When we pray, we 'send' our prayer to God." Fly the airplane.
"But did you know that when we pray, our prayers never miss their
destination? They *always* reach God's ears. He always hears our
prayers, no matter if it's day or night, no matter if we pray out loud or

silently in our hearts." You may also want to share a Scripture passage that communicates this truth, such as Psalm 34:15, 17 or Proverbs 15:29.

Invite your child to silently "say" a prayer as you both throw your airplanes one more time, imagining that you're "sending" your prayers to God.

exploration

You may want to ask your child questions like these:

* How does it feel to know God always hears your prayers, no matter what?
* I love to pray for you and to talk to God about what's going on in your life. Are there things you'd like me to pray about?

bonus!

If you want to try out a variety of paper airplane styles with your kids, check out this Web site with twenty-four different designs: http://www.paperairplanes.co.uk.

basic paper airplane instructions

1. Fold the paper in half lengthwise.
2. At one end, fold the open corners down until they are aligned with the first fold, forming a point.
3. Fold those edges back again, aligning them with the first fold.
4. Repeat that same step one final time.
5. Grab the center, fold the wings out, and glide it through the air.

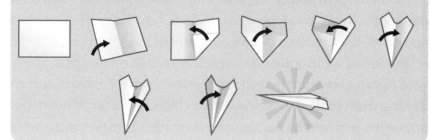

*Create bubble solution together to help
your child understand what it means
to be filled with the Spirit.*

experience

Use this simple recipe (on the following page) to create an amazing, homemade bubble solution with your child. Then have a blast blowing great big bubbles together.

supplies:
- bubble wands
- water
- dish soap
- glycerin
- sugar
- measuring cups and spoons
- jar or bottle

connection

As you gently blow into your bubble wand and fill the solution with air to create a floating, shiny, beautiful bubble, invite your child to think first about how God "breathed" life into the very first human, Adam (Gen. 2:7). Then explain how the same thing happens in our lives when we put our faith in Jesus: God fills us with the life-giving Holy Spirit. Share with your child that God desires us to "be filled with the Spirit" (Eph. 5:18) and to "live by the Spirit" (Gal. 5:16). You may also want to share Galatians 5:25, which reads, "Since we are living by the Spirit, let us follow the Spirit's leading in every part of our lives" (NLT). Like the "magic" of air invisibly filling bubbles and causing them to float, God's Spirit works invisibly inside of us to give us true life: joy, meaning, direction, and hope.

exploration

You may want to ask your child questions like these:

❋ Can you see or feel the Holy Spirit? What is the Holy Spirit like?

❋ How does the Holy Spirit fill us up? How is it like or unlike the way our breath fills up the bubbles?

❋ What wonderful things does the Holy Spirit do in our lives?

super-power bubble mix

ingredients

- 1 c. water
- 2 tbsp. liquid dish-washing detergent
- 1 tbsp. glycerin (available in the baking aisle at grocery stores and at pharmacies)
- 1 tsp. sugar

In a bowl, mix together the water, glycerin, and soap. Then stir in the sugar until it has completely dissolved. Pour your solution into a bottle or jar. Use a wand to start blowing amazing bubbles!

in the light : **30**

Use a glow-in-the-dark toy to help your child understand what it means to abide in Christ and be close to him.

experience

Gather one or more glow-in-the-dark toys and explain to your child that for the toys to brightly glow, they need to spend some time near a lamp (or in the sun), soaking up the light. Pick a bright light in your house together, turn it on, and arrange the toys in the light. Let the toys sit under the light for at least five minutes. (If you're able, leave them there for an hour or more while you and your child do other things.)

After the toys have had time to charge up with light, have your child help you take them into a completely darkened room (such as a bathroom without any windows) and enjoy watching them glow.

supplies:
- one (or more) glow-in-the-dark toy
- a bright lamp

connection

This is a powerful picture of what happens when we spend time with Jesus. Use this experience to help your child think about what it means for us to be close to Jesus—to be in his light (1 John 1:7). You may want to repeat the activity, talking with your child about the spiritual meaning as you wait a few minutes for the toys to soak up light once more. Ask your child about experiences he's had or things he does that help him feel close to God, and share about some of your own spiritual-growth habits such as prayer, worship, and Bible reading. Emphasize to your child that God wants him to be close to him all the time! You may also want to read John 15:4. Jesus' words here are translated many different ways, including "Remain in me" (NIV, NLT), "Abide in me" (KJV, ESV), "Live in me" (MSG), and "Dwell in me" (AB). Help your child understand the simple picture here: just as the toy is in the light, soaking it up, so we can be in Christ's light. And as we spend time close to Jesus, we glow with his light and love to the world around us.

As you take the toys into the darkened room again, pray aloud together, thanking God for helping both of you glow with his love.

exploration

You may want to ask your child questions like these:

✻ When have you felt really close to God?
✻ What are some things you like to do to be close to God?
✻ How do you think God wants you to "glow" in this world?

an invisible (not imaginary) friend **31**

Spend a day talking out loud to God as if he's there in the room. (After all, he is!)

experience

Many young children have imaginary friends whom they talk to, out loud, on a regular basis. Those who don't have "long-term" imaginary friends still often invent them for play scenarios, giving voices to characters, toys, or other imaginary

supplies:
• none

characters. But does your child realize she truly does have an invisible friend who's always there, ready to listen?

Start out the day with your child by saying something like, "Today we're going to pray to God a lot. But we're not going to bow our heads or close our eyes or fold our hands. We're just going to *talk* to him . . . out loud!"

This will feel a bit silly and will generate laughs and smiles, but that's part of the fun! Set an example here as you say spontaneous out-loud prayers to God (within your child's earshot) throughout the day. You could say really meaningful things out of the blue, like, "God, I love you so much!" or "God, thank you for protecting our family and keeping us safe." Or you could pray about more random things, like, "God, you made that robin in our backyard. He's cool!" or "Mm, this hot cocoa is good. Thanks for inventing marshmallows, God!"

connection

Setting aside time for prayer is a wonderful habit, and those times of focused communication with God are really important. But when we focus too much on a set-aside time for prayer, we often regretfully neglect the other 23.5 hours of the day! Just as Paul urged the Thessalonians, we can train our children to "pray continually" (1 Thess. 5:17). Modeling spontaneous, out-loud prayer is a powerful way of communicating some critical truths to your child: We can talk to God any time, any place, and for any reason. We can keep our attention on him throughout the day (not just at bedtime). We believe he's right here with us and he cares about even the littlest details of our lives.

Literally "praying continually" is not really possible—after all, we must sleep! But we can all certainly pray more than we do, and we can establish a rhythm of prayer in our lives that stretches throughout each day. This rhythm of continuous prayer can come about as we develop a variety of types of prayer in our lives (and our children's lives), such as spontaneous prayer, breath prayer, meditation, singing prayers, coloring prayers, and more. It's easy and fun to pray spontaneously throughout each day; and by praying out loud so your child can hear, you invite her into your prayer and you inspire her to pick up the habit.

exploration

You may want to ask your child questions like these:

* What does it feel like to talk out loud to God? Why?
* How do you most like to pray? With eyes closed and head bowed? Out loud with eyes open? Some other way? Why?
* Prayer can look different and people can do it different ways. How would you define what prayer really is?
* What's the point of praying? Why do we do it?

keep in step 32

*Make footprints in the snow to inspire your
child to walk "in step" with God's Spirit.*

experience

On a wintry day when snow has freshly fallen,
bundle up with your child for a fun game in the
yard. Create a footprint path that meanders
around, matching the length of a child's stride.
Eventually lead your path back to where you
started. When you're both done, invite your child

supplies:
- snow boots
- winter coats
- snow pants

to join you as you try to walk together along the same path (with
your child in the lead). Say, "Let's follow the footprints exactly. Try
to place your feet right in my footprints!" If your child likes this
game, try it again in a new, undisturbed area of freshly fallen snow.
Challenge your child to make the path this time and to make it even
tougher to follow.

Playing in the snow is one of the best parts of winter for kids who
live in the northern half of the country. Along with snow angels,
snowmen, and snowball fights, creating footprint paths in the snow
is about as natural to a child as can be. Adding this extra step of
retracing the paths turns them into a game. Trust me, it's not as
easy as it sounds! If the snow is deep, you'll both end up falling over
several times!

connection

As you're retracing a path together, share briefly with your child that there's a Bible verse that encourages us to "keep in step with the Spirit" (Gal. 5:25). Say something simple like, "God's Spirit guides us and changes us and shows us how to live. Just like we're walking in these footprints, we can try to line up every step we take in life exactly with how God's Spirit is leading us." Then, unless your child is burning to talk further, table this discussion and have fun playing.

When you're done playing and you've come inside to take off your coats and boots, remind your child of the footprint path and ask, "Was that game easy or hard? Why?" Share Galatians 5:25 and invite your child to share his thoughts about what the verse means. You might also want to share with your child Job's description of his efforts to live a godly life: "I've followed him closely, my feet in his footprints, not once swerving from his way" (Job 23:11 MSG).

Invite your child to imagine two different ways of living. In one way, people just make their own path, wandering around on their own. In the other way, people follow the path given to them by God—they follow God closely, taking steps right in the footprints he's made for them. Talk together about how a person lives the second way, following in God's steps. Then pray aloud very briefly for your child, asking God to help him daily keep in step with God's Spirit.

exploration

You may want to ask your child questions like these:

* What do you think it means to "keep in step" with God's Spirit?
* Imagine a person who keeps in step with God's Spirit. What is that person like? How does that person act?
* Do you think it's easy or hard to "keep in step" with God's Spirit?
* Job used footprints to describe following God closely. How *does* a person follow God closely? What habits help us live like that?

life on the farm 33

*Visit a farm with your child to help her consider
what it takes to tend to one's spiritual life.*

experience

Plan a visit to a nearby family farm, ideally one
that raises livestock as well as veggies, grains, or other
produce. Arrange with the farmer to get a tour of
his farm and learn with your child about all the work
the farmer does on a daily basis to help the food grow and to keep the
animals healthy. See if your child can get up close to some of the farm
animals, help pour feed into a trough, and walk along some rows of
corn or growing wheat. Ask the farmer to describe what he and his
family members do on a typical day to run the farm. It's hard work!

supplies:
• none

Be sure to thank the farmer for his time by purchasing some of his
produce, eggs, or meat or by paying him for the tour.

connection

Visiting a farm is tons of fun, particularly for city kids or
suburbanites. But it also puts things into perspective: Crops don't just
grow on their own! Farmers need to do constant work to tend to
their crops and livestock: feeding and fertilizing; preventing disease
and caring for the sick; harvesting, milking, and egg collecting; and
so much more.

As you drive home from the farm, recall together all the tasks a farm family does to keep things running smoothly. Then ask, "What would happen to the farm if they didn't do those things?" Help your child elaborate on this idea by really thinking through the consequences: Eggs and milk wouldn't be collected, grain wouldn't be harvested. But even worse, the animals would eventually die and the crops would wither away!

Next, draw a comparison between a functioning farm and a person's spiritual life. You could say, "Just like that farmer has to do a lot of work to tend to his farm, God wants us to tend to our spiritual lives. God wants us to do the work we need to do to keep growing spiritually." Pray briefly together, asking God to show you ways he might want you to do some "hard work" to keep your spiritual life healthy and growing.

exploration

You may want to ask your child questions like these:

* ✻ Imagine you were a farmer. Which of the farmer's jobs would you most want to do? Which of his jobs would you least want to do? Why?
* ✻ How is running a farm like a person's spiritual life? How is it different?
* ✻ What are some things we need to do to tend to our spiritual lives?
* ✻ If people just sit idly by and don't tend to their spiritual lives, what can happen?
* ✻ If a person does tend to his spiritual life, what will happen? How will that person grow? How will that person change?

bonus!

Not sure where to find a farm to visit? Check out the www.localharvest.org search engine to locate some family farms.

Use a silly family adventure to help your child understand what it means to follow God's direction in his life.

experience

Load up the family into the car and explain how this fun adventure will work. At each stoplight or stop sign, one of the family members will shout out "right," "left," or "straight." The driver then follows that instruction. At the next stop, another family member gets to shout out a direction. Everyone continues to take turns until you reach a destination, a dead-end, or wind up in the middle of nowhere—at which point you can start the game over again.

supplies:
- the family car
- map (optional)
- money for treats (optional)

Do your best to finagle things so that you finally wind up at a spot where you can buy treats, such as an ice cream shop or a gas station stocked with candy. And, if needed, use a map to find your way home again.

connection

As you drive home, talk about the adventure you just went on together, emphasizing the sense of the unknown and the feelings of surprise and curiosity you all experienced. Talk together about how following God's lead in our lives can feel like that sometimes—God tells us to go in a certain direction, but we may have no idea how it will turn out or where we'll end up!

We don't always know where God is leading us, but we can trust him and obey his direction because he has our best interests at heart. If you'd like, share with your child the truths found in Proverbs 3:5–6 and consider telling him about a time when you obeyed God's direction even though you were uncertain about how things would turn out.

exploration

You may want to ask your child questions like these:

* What was the best part of our trip? The scariest? The most uncertain?
* Where did you think we'd end up? Were you surprised? Why or why not?
* Did you know God gives us direction in life? We don't usually hear him say "Turn left!"—but we may feel in our hearts or learn from the Bible something he wants us to do. What kinds of directions has God given to you?
* Do you think it's easy or hard to obey God and follow his direction for our lives? Explain.

*Use a bottle of soda to celebrate
God with your child, turning your
worship into overflowing joy!*

experience

On a warm day, take your child outside for a
silly time of celebration focused on who God is.

supplies:
• 1 bottle of
  soda

Take turns shaking the soda bottle. As you each
shake it, shout out to God things you love about
him, like, "God, you are good!" or "Jesus, you are my best friend!"
or "God, you created me!" Be sure to have a big smile on your own
face and an excited tone of voice—your example will help your child
get into the activity, expressing real happiness and authentic joy.
Keep shaking the bottle and naming things until your arms are
exhausted and you're laughing and having fun together.

Then shout out together, "God, our joy is overflowing!" Aim the
soda bottle away from your child as you open it and the soda sprays
out all over the place.

connection

Plop down on the ground together and laugh about what you
just experienced. Then share with your child about how important
it is to celebrate God and to have overflowing joy in our hearts.
You may want to share David's words in Psalm 119:171 or Paul's

description of overflowing joy and thanks in 2 Corinthians 4:15; 8:2; 9:12; and Colossians 2:6–7. If your child enjoys this experience, make it a habit to celebrate God this way often!

exploration

You may want to ask your child questions like these:

❋ What do you think it means to have overflowing joy?

❋ What things about God give you the most joy?

❋ How can we show that joy to each other? What can we do to fill our house with joy?

Make a special picture frame to help your child zero in on a specific prayer focus each week.

experience

Invite your child to create a "prayer portrait" frame to hang on your refrigerator. To make the frame, help your child affix craft sticks in a rectangular shape; he can make the frame as big or small as he'd like. The frame itself should be at least two sticks wide so there's a sufficient surface to decorate. Your child can use regular liquid glue to put the frame together (allow about an hour to dry before decorating), or you can use a hot glue gun (allow about ten minutes for it to cool).

Once the frame is set, help your child decorate it any way he'd like, such as coloring the wood with markers or gluing objects to every inch of its surface. Simply encourage your child to make it special. After all the glue has dried again, affix magnets all over the back of the frame.

supplies:
- adhesive magnets (available at craft and office supply stores)
- craft sticks (tongue depressors)
- glue
- decorations (such as sequins, glitter glue, fuzz balls, yarn, markers, foam shapes, feathers, or buttons)
- markers
- hot glue gun (optional)

connection

Prayer can feel very abstract to children—it's talking (sometimes silently) to an invisible God about invisible thoughts and invisible feelings. Using a prayer portrait can provide a concrete, three-dimensional focus for a young child as he seeks to learn the habit of prayer. Each week, help your child think of one specific person or need he wants to pray for. For example, your child may want to pray for his grandparents, so you can put a photograph of them on the fridge and use the frame to keep it in place. Or perhaps your child might want to pray for something more general like, "I want to pray for kids who are poor." Help your child draw a picture of needy children and write the words of your child's prayer at the bottom. Put the "portrait" in the frame on the refrigerator.

Start a habit of a short daily time of prayer for whoever is featured in the prayer portrait, such as during afternoon snack time. With the picture right in front of your child as a concrete visual cue, prompt him to pray aloud or silently (while you join in or take the lead) for the person or need featured there. And guess what? He can keep his eyes open, looking right at the image as he prays!

exploration

You may want to ask your child questions like these:

* Whom do you think we should pray for each day this week? What should we pray about as we talk to God about that person (or issue)?
* Why do you want to pray for that person (or about that issue)?

Bake and eat pretzels together to learn about different postures for prayer.

experience

Pretzels are a delicious treat—especially when they're freshly baked. But did you know that pretzels have a spiritual history? Legend has it that pretzels were first created by a monk in the 600s as a way of teaching young children to pray.

supplies:
- ingredients (see below)
- kitchen tools

In that time period, Christians didn't fold their hands and bow their heads to pray; instead they prayed with arms folded across the chest, with hands on opposite shoulders. When you look at the shape of a pretzel, you can see right away how this simple way of shaping bread was used to represent the posture for prayer. From that time on, pretzels were eaten during Lent to symbolize the focus on prayer and devotion during that season.

Get your child involved in making the pretzels. An older child can help throughout the whole recipe, while a younger child may enjoy being involved only at the end—rolling the dough and shaping the pretzels.

delicious homemade pretzels

ingredients

pretzels
- 1½ c. warm water (test it on your wrist to make sure it's warm, not hot)
- 4 tsp. active dry yeast
- 1 tsp. white sugar
- 4 c. white flour
- 1 c. whole wheat flour
- ½ c. white sugar
- 1½ tsp. salt
- 2 tbsp. vegetable oil

toppings
- melted butter
- kosher salt
- cinnamon sugar
- garlic salt
- sesame oil
- sesame seeds

pretzel bath
- ½ c. baking soda
- 4 c. hot water

Mix yeast and 1 tsp. sugar into the warm water. Let it stand 5–10 minutes until creamy.

Meanwhile, stir together the flours, sugar, and salt. When the yeast mixture is ready, pour it in along with the oil and stir to mix. When it's too difficult to mix with a spoon, mix it with your hands. Knead the dough for 7–10 minutes. As you knead, if the dough seems too stiff or dry, dip your hands in water and knead it in. Repeat as necessary.

Form the dough into a ball and place it in an oiled bowl, turning the dough to coat it.

Cover the bowl with plastic wrap and let it rise in a warm place until it has doubled in size—about 1 to 1½ hours.

Once the dough has risen adequately, prepare the pretzel bath by dissolving the baking soda in the hot water. (Put the mixture in dish big enough to hold an individual pretzel.) Also, preheat your oven to 450 degrees.

Punch down the dough, loosely shape it into a ball, and put it on a floured surface. Cut the ball into 12 roughly even pieces. One at a time, roll the pieces into "snakes" and then form into a pretzel shape. Keep the rest of the pieces covered with a damp cloth while you work.

Once you've formed 12 pretzels, dip them one at a time into the "pretzel bath." Then place on a greased baking sheet. (If you like salty pretzels, sprinkle kosher salt on them at this point.) Bake the pretzels for about 7–9 minutes until browned.

If you'd like to put toppings on your pretzels, it's best to do so right when they come out of the oven. Two of our favorite topping combos are brushing the pretzel with melted butter then sprinkling with cinnamon sugar; or, brushing the pretzel with sesame oil then topping with sesame seeds.

connection

As you form the pretzels, invite your child to make a "pretzel" shape with her arms, folding them across the chest and placing her hands on opposite shoulders. Share with your child the story of how pretzels were first created. Then pray together in this ancient posture before you eat.

While you eat, talk with your child about various postures for prayer mentioned in the Bible, such as lying down flat on the ground (1 Kings 18:39), bowing (Ps. 5:7), kneeling (Ps. 95:6), or lifting up hands (Ps. 63:4). Encourage your child to be free and creative with prayer, expressing herself to God both verbally and physically.

exploration

You may want to ask your child questions like these:

* What did it feel like to pray in a different way? Why?
* Do you think it matters to God what posture you're in when you pray? Why or why not?
* How can you use the position of your body to express feelings to God?
* Do you think you may want to try out a new posture for prayer sometime? If so, which one?

bonus!

The fun children's book *Walter the Baker* by Eric Carle tells a fictitious story about the invention of pretzels. On the very last page, however, Carle recounts the true origin of pretzels. Read this story together at bedtime as a way to cap off a fun day!

38 pulling soul-weeds

Pull weeds with your child to discover the importance of confession.

supplies:
- gardening gloves (optional)
- shovels and spades
- bucket

experience

Recruit your child to help you pull weeds from your garden or flowerbed; what seems like an annoying task for you is often pretty fun for kids! Start out by kneeling down together and helping your child visually distinguish the weeds from the good plants. Then show your child how to grab the weed at its base, pull it up (roots and all), and toss it in a bucket.

Have fun working together, being sure to *ooh* and *ah* whenever your child gets a big one. And don't worry if he doesn't do it quite right! Thank him for his help, no matter what.

connection

When you're done working, discuss weed-pulling as a metaphor for the way we need to deal with sin in our lives. Say something like, "Our lives can be a lot like our garden. They can be full of good things, but there are usually also weeds that sneak in. The weeds are sins in our lives, like selfishness or lying or disobedience or saying mean things. If we let those weeds stay, they'll take root and grow and really mess up the garden! God wants us to do our part to keep those weeds out. He's given us a way to weed out those sins that sneak into our lives and it's called 'confession.' Confession is when we recognize sins and tell God we're sorry for them. When we do that, it's like God yanks those sins right out! He forgives us!"

It's important here to communicate theological truth clearly: Ultimately it is *God* who does the work of forgiving and not us. Christ's redemptive work on the cross is more than sufficient to forgive every sin we ever have and ever will commit! But part of spiritual maturation is the willingness to look closely at our lives and honestly identify the sins we've committed. When we name and confess our specific sins (rather than asking for a general forgiveness), we claim Christ's power to help us overcome them. Scripture repeatedly affirms the importance of this spiritual practice in passages such as Psalm 32:1–5 and 1 John 1:9.

Living in private guilt is a painful thing for both grown-ups and children. Model simple and regular prayers of confession for your child. As this becomes a habit for him, he'll be better able to approach God in confession during those times of serious guilt and shame. He'll know from experience that God hears his prayer and yanks that weed right out, forgiving him fully and completely.

exploration

You may want to ask your child questions like these:

* What did you like about pulling weeds? (Or what didn't you like?)
* How important is it to pull weeds? How often do you think we should weed our garden so the weeds don't take over?
* What are some sin-weeds that can sneak into people's lives?
* Why is it important to pull those sin-weeds right out? What can happen if we just let them grow in our lives?

39 silent sunrise

Take in a lovely sunrise with your child to help her experience silent worship.

supplies:
- lawn chairs (optional)
- hot cocoa (optional)

experience

In the spring or fall, when sunrises aren't *super* early, watch the weather predictions for an upcoming clear or slightly cloudy day and schedule in some time in the morning for watching the sunrise together. (Check the time of sunrise in your local paper; it will tell you when the first part of the sun will peek above the horizon. Of course, the brilliant colors appear before that time, so plan to be outside at least five minutes before the actual sunrise.)

Invite your child to watch something beautiful with you. Then set up lawn chairs in the yard and see God's artistry in action. If it's cold out, bring out some toasty mugs of hot cocoa to sip together. Then say, "Let's just be quiet together as we watch God paint the sky. Let's worship him in our hearts."

connection

OK, OK, it probably isn't realistic to expect your child to be completely quiet for ten minutes. My kids wouldn't be able to last more than about thirty seconds before whispering something! But *aiming* for quietness, modeling it, and helping your child be quiet for spans and spurts during this experience will help her experience and gain familiarity with two important spiritual disciplines: silence and worship.

The amount of time your child is quiet during this activity isn't as important as what she'll feel as she steps away from media and routine with you for ten minutes focused on God's glory in nature. When we focus on a sunrise, we can't help but be struck by God's awesomeness! And for a child, taking that in with eyes open and mouth (temporarily) closed will prompt thoughts, feelings, and inner reflection about the beauty of this world and God's majesty.

When the sunrise is nearly complete, say something like, "Isn't it special to worship God in this way—quietly and from our hearts? Thank you, God, for this beautiful sunrise."

exploration

You may want to ask your child questions like these:

* What did you think of that sunrise? How would you describe it?
* What did it show us about God?
* Did it help you feel close to God? Explain.
* What was it like to worship God quietly? What did you like about it? What was challenging about it?

40 tv turn-off week

Fast from television together as an act of devotion to God.

supplies:
• none

experience

Fasting is a spiritual growth practice that's emphasized in both the Old and New Testaments. For many of us it may seem optional, but Jesus spoke about fasting as a normative part of a growing spiritual life. (See Matt. 6:16, in which Jesus said, *"when* you fast" not *"if* you fast," emphasis added.) Though fasting from food isn't a good idea for children because of their nutritional needs, there's another important way you can fast: by giving up TV and video games as a family.

Decide on a week (or longer) that can be your family's TV turn-off week. Talk about it well in advance so everyone can be mentally prepared and emotionally onboard with the plan. Then dive in! Cover your TVs with bed sheets and replace TV-watching time with family activities like reading, going on walks, playing board games, doing crafts, talking, serving others, or worshiping God through songs and prayer.

connection

There are plenty of good reasons to turn off the TV. It's a break from materialistic messages sent through advertisements. It will cause your child to develop his imagination and resourcefulness as he comes up with other things to do. It will increase personal interaction among family members.

But the core reason for this TV turn-off week needs to be clear: It's a *fast*. This means you're choosing to give something up for God, almost as if you're giving him a gift. Before the TV turn-off week starts, talk with your child about what fasting means. Explain that whenever we fast, it's going to "hurt" a little bit. After all, if we gave up something that was "easy" (like broccoli), it wouldn't really count as a fast because it's not a meaningful sacrifice. Giving up TV will be a challenge, and that's what makes the fast significant.

When negative feelings arise during your turn-off week, remind your child (and yourself) that this is an act of worship and redirect your "hunger" for TV toward a spiritual hunger for God. Connect the dots clearly for your child by leading him in prayer during those times, saying, "God, it's hard for us not to watch TV right now because we're used to doing it. We really *want* to watch TV, but, God, we want you more and we love you more. We're choosing not to watch TV right now as a way of reminding ourselves and showing you that we love you more than anything else."

exploration

You may want to ask your child questions like these:

* What was the hardest part about our TV fast? What was the best part?
* What did you learn from this experience?
* What do you think fasting means? Why do we fast?
* What other kinds of fasts might you want to do in the future?

41 up-close examination

View your home through a magnifying glass to introduce the discipline of examen.

supplies:
- powerful magnifying glass

experience

Show your child how to correctly use a magnifying glass. Then troop around the house together examining objects in your house up close. Check out things that will look interesting when magnified, like carpet fibers, textured paint, tennis shoe soles, sparkly jewelry, crumbs, fingerprints on the windows, furry stuffed animals, torn paper, a dollar bill, and the text in a book. You could also have your child use the magnifying glass to look at parts of his body (wrinkles on his skin, his toenail, his eye via a mirror) or nature in the backyard (blades of grass, a chunk of dirt, an insect). When you're done examining things, talk about what your child observed, particularly things he might not have noticed if he wasn't looking up close.

connection

David passionately prayed, "Search me, O God, and know my heart; test me and know my anxious thoughts. See if there is any offensive way in me, and lead me in the way everlasting" (Ps. 139:23–24). One of the most important spiritual practices you can teach your child is inviting God to search his life through prayerful self-examination.

Ignatius of Loyola outlined a five-step process called *examen*, and many Christians throughout history have taught various other methods for self-examination. To put it simply, *examen* is when we join God in putting a magnifying glass on our lives, looking closely and honestly at our day through spiritual eyes. For a child, this can be as simple as taking just a few minutes to reflect together at bedtime, inviting your child to consider a time during the day when he may not have been close to God or been following God's desires and also to think of a time when he connected with God or observed God's power and love.

On the day you've done the magnifying glass activity, set aside a few minutes at bedtime to share Psalm 139:23–24 with your child. Explain, "We should also ask God to search us—to look up close at our lives. And we can join him in that, looking at our days with a spiritual magnifying glass." Model this by sharing a time from your day when you feel, upon reflection, that you sinned or neglected your relationship with God. Be sure to also share a few positive observations, such as a time when you obeyed God and a time when you worshiped God. Then use the questions below to help your child to do the same.

exploration

You may want to ask your child questions like these:

* What was the high point (or best part) of your day today? How was God a part of it?
* What was the low point (or worst part) of your day today? How was God a part of it?
* When you examine your day up close, do you see any parts of it in which God showed you his love? Do you see times you showed God's love to others?
* When you look up close at your day, do you see times when you sinned, ignored God, or were far away from him in your thoughts or actions?
* How do you want to serve God and be close to him tomorrow?

42 what are you seeking?

*Play Memory and help your child consider
what it really means to seek God.*

supplies:
- Memory (by Milton Bradley)

experience

Play several rounds of Memory with your child. In this classic game, players turn over cards to try to find matching pairs. As the game gets rolling, players use their memories to seek out and find the correct cards. As you play, draw attention to the searching aspect of the game as you each look at the array of facedown cards and try to find cards that match. Say simple things like, "I'm searching . . . I'm searching . . . I know I'm going to find the card I want!" or "Do you think you'll be able to find the card you're seeking?" Be sure to verbally celebrate with your child each time she completes a pair, saying, "Good work searching. You found it!"

connection

For many people in our world, God seems elusive. They feel they have to search for God through various personal journeys into different philosophies, religions, books, and even exercise classes. Many people also search for "God" within themselves. Sadly, many of them feel very little hope of ever finding this mysterious deity, *if* he (or she) even exists.

But we know the truth—and it's amazing. God is anything but elusive! In his Word, he makes this promise to his people: "But if from there you seek the LORD your God, you will find him if you look for him with all your heart and with all your soul" (Deut. 4:29). This promise is repeated many times throughout Scripture, such as in Jeremiah 29:13, which says, "You will seek me and find me when you seek me with all your heart." God desires that we "find" him! But there's something essential in these passages that's often overlooked in our culture of easy, instant answers: We must *seek* God with our heart and soul—with our whole being.

Use the Memory game to talk with your child about these verses and to explore with her what it means to seek God. Share with your child some of the methods Christians use to grow spiritually and to seek after God—prayer, worship, study of Scripture, giving, fasting, and other spiritual disciplines. Say something like, "When we played this game, we each put our full focus into trying to find the cards we wanted. Now imagine focusing like that on God. Now imagine doubling that focus and effort. Now imagine tripling it! Really, we should seek after God with so much focus and passion and desire that our efforts to search in this game pale in comparison!"

exploration

You may want to ask your child questions like these:

✻ What do you think it means to seek God or to search for God?
✻ What do you think it means to "find" God?
✻ What does it look like to seek God? What do Christians do to seek God?
✻ How much heart and soul do you put into seeking God? How much do you *want* to put into seeking God?

with all your mind : part 3

*planting the seed
of God's word*

Ever heard someone share a testimony something like this?

"See, I used to just have head knowledge about God . . ." (the speaker points to his head) ". . . but then I realized I needed to know and love Jesus in my heart!" (the speaker points to his heart).

> "Love the Lord your God . . . with all your mind."
> —Jesus (Mark 12:30)

The core idea here is true: Intellectual knowledge about a subject does not equal faith.

But this supposed head and heart dichotomy—this view of intellectual learning as anti-faith—is a fallacy! Intellectual learning is an *essential* aspect of faith. Jesus himself invited us to love God with our minds; and it seems to me that to know more about God naturally leads us to love him all the more.

So what does it mean to love God with one's mind? In some senses, any type of learning, be it about science or mathematics or literature, can be a way of loving God with one's mind. But the foundational way to love God with one's mind is to engage the intellect in learning about God through his Word.

this ain't school

Let's get one thing straight before we move on: *God* and *boring* are two words that should never be paired together in your child's mind! The goal of this section is to give you tools and ideas for moving beyond (*way* beyond) the Sunday school methods of old that drummed verses into children's brains with endless repetition and that quizzed them on essentially meaningless Bible facts. Didactically cramming knowledge into a child's brain will *not* result in life change. But learning that's engaging and fun and that's driven by a vibrant, living, and active relationship with God will give your child a solid foundation for life.

God created our brains and he knows a thing or two about how they work. He designed learning to be exciting—to involve our senses, to invite our questions, to invigorate our faith (rather than bore it to death!). Your responsibility in nurturing the intellectual aspect of your child's faith is twofold. First, your aim is to teach your child the truths of God's Word. And second, your task is to teach your child to *love* God's Word. And with a few tips from Jesus, you'll find that neither task is difficult to accomplish.

tips from Jesus

the power of story

Throughout the centuries and across all cultures, one thing has always been true: Children *love* a good story. They love to imagine a character making her way through life, facing conflicts, dealing with plot twists, and hopefully making it out OK in the end. When a young man asked him, "Who is my neighbor," Jesus could have simply said, "Every person is your neighbor." But instead he told a story—a haunting, compelling, intriguing story that strikes right at the heart of the human experience. We know it as the parable of the Good Samaritan.

Through story, Jesus spoke right to the heart. Through unforgettable stories, Jesus communicated unforgettable truths.

One of the most important ways you can plant a love for God's Word in your child's heart is to begin with the stories. From your child's earliest age, tell him the stories of God's people. Tell him about Adam and Eve; Joseph and his brothers; Moses; David and Goliath; Shadrach, Meshach, and Abednego. Describe for him Peter walking on the water out to Jesus; the women discovering Christ's empty tomb; Paul and Silas singing in prison. Through storybooks and Scripture reading, through pantomime and puppet shows, through after-church chats and breakfast discussions, you can infuse your child's life with the amazing stories recorded in God's Word. The stories of God's people can serve as a framework for your child, leading and guiding the way he lives out his own life story.

ordinary objects, extraordinary truths

Coins. Bread. Salt. Sand. Fishing. Building. Farming.

These are just a few of the common objects and first-century experiences Jesus transformed into vehicles of eternal truth. He was the master of metaphor! His teachings were infused with word pictures layered with meaning. And Jesus' example models for us one of the very best ways we as parents can bring God's Word to life for our children: by turning the common objects and experiences of their lives (like snacks and toys and games) into powerful symbols of biblical truth.

This section is packed with ideas for using objects and experiences to function as symbols for Bible verses and theological ideas. You can also take this approach and run with it—don't limit yourself to the specific suggestions in this section. Use some of the obvious pointers Scripture gives you to pair a hands-on symbol or experience with your child's Bible learning. For example, you could eat bread with your child while you talk about the feeding of the five thousand (Matt. 14). You could make a sheep out of cotton balls and glue as you talk about God as our shepherd (Ps. 23). You could dig in the dirt to explore Jesus' parable of the seeds (Mark 4).

In addition to the metaphors the Bible already provides, you can also get your creative wheels turning and come up with ways to create spiritual symbols out of household items on your own. Think of a unique object or a favorite recipe or a much-loved game and brainstorm about how it might be used to communicate an eternal truth. You'll be surprised to discover how much meaning can be packed into an old tennis shoe, a sandbox, a sock monkey, or a jumbo marshmallow!

my brain ♥'s God

In the next several pages you'll find ideas for ways to explore specific Bible verses and theological ideas, and you'll also find suggestions for kid-friendly practices and habits that will nurture a growing, lifelong love for learning God's Word. You can draw out an intellectual love for God and his Word in your child that integrates your child's God-given gifts of memory, rationality, exploration, and examination with the love pouring forth from his heart and his soul.

and the winner is . . . **43**

Race toy cars across the kitchen floor . . .
and learn something about the kingdom
of God in the process.

experience

Clear the furniture out of the way and lie
down on your belly with your child for some
intense car racing, complete with sound effects!
The idea is simple: Line up the cars, identify
who is racing which cars, shout "Go," and give
your cars a shove! You can decide together if the winner is the car
that goes the farthest or the car that passes a designated finish
line first. Ham it up with buzzing lip motor sounds and lots of
cheering for the winners. Play several rounds of this, being sure to
emphasize (with your child's help) which cars have won or lost
each race. (And by the way, be sure your cars lose just as much as
your child's cars.)

supplies:
• toy cars

connection

Sometimes Jesus said the wackiest, most counterintuitive things.
And perhaps one of his most against-the-grain teachings is this one:
"If anyone wants to be first, he must be the very last, and the servant
of all" (Mark 9:35). Could anything seem less logical, less natural?
Even one-year-olds understand our human penchant for self-centered

competition, striving to grab something first or to hoard something all to oneself.

This fun playtime is a great avenue for introducing your child to the challenging idea that things work much differently in God's kingdom than they do in regular life. After one of your races (and raucous, enthusiastic declarations of winners and losers), you could say something like, "Did you know Jesus talked about what it means to be first and last? And he said something really unusual." Share Mark 9:35 with your child (or Matt. 20:16, which puts it this way: "The last will be first, and the first will be last").

Invite your child to remark about what he thinks Jesus meant. Then briefly share the idea of servant-like actions—of voluntarily being "last"—in terms your child will understand. For example, a person could be "last" by letting his sister pick a cookie first during snack time or by opening a door for others and holding it so they can pass through first.

To keep your child engaged, don't belabor the conversation—get back to racing cars. But to reinforce the point, try a few silly races by saying something like, "Let's see who can get across the finish line *last* this time."

exploration

You may want to ask your child questions like these:

* What do you think Jesus might have meant when he said to be first we need to be last?
* What are some ways people in our family can be "last" and serve each other?
* What are some ways of serving others that you like or want to try?

asleep on the hay **44**

Bake yummy cookies together to represent Jesus' first cradle: a manger.

experience

Your family may have favorite Christmas cookie recipes, but "Manger Cookies" (usually called "haystacks") carry a special meaning your child is sure to love all year round.

supplies:
- ingredients (see below)
- kitchen tools

connection

When the King of the universe came to earth, it wasn't to a throne or a castle. In fact, Luke 2:3 tells us that the infant Jesus had a manger as his first cradle. Unless you live on a farm, it's likely that your child has never seen anything remotely like a manger and only uses the word when singing Christmas carols. So take a moment to talk simply about what a manger is: a feeding trough for livestock like cattle or horses. It's basically just a box filled with hay or other feed. Explain to your child that the cookies you're about to make look like haystacks—the same type of material that likely served as Jesus' first mattress when he was just hours old.

As you bake together, you may want to emphasize the humility of Jesus' birth by contrasting it with the setting in which your child was born: in a clean hospital, with a doctor to help, and with nice warm blankets to snuggle in. Whether it's Christmastime or summer vacation, you can make and eat these manger cookies together to help your child learn about Jesus' birth in a memorable way.

exploration

You may want to ask your child questions like these:

✻ What do you think your birth was like? What do you think your first cradle was like?

✻ Imagine you're a mom who's just given birth to your first baby. (Or imagine you're a dad and your wife has just given birth to your first baby.) Would you want to place your baby in a manger? Why or why not?

✻ Why do you think God chose to come into the world this way?

manger cookies

ingredients

- 1 c. butterscotch chips
- ½ c. peanut butter
- 2 c. chow mein noodles
- 1 c. mini-marshmallows
- ¼ c. milk chocolate chips
- ½ c. coconut flakes (optional)

You'll need to work quickly once you start this recipe, so ready all your ingredients ahead of time. First, put 1 c. butterscotch chips and ½ c. peanut butter into a large microwavable bowl. In a second bowl, place your "hay" ingredients: 2 c. chow mein noodles and ½ c. coconut flakes. (You may omit the coconut if desired.) In a third bowl place your extras: 1 c. mini-marshmallows and ¼ c. chocolate chips. Last, spread sheets of wax paper (or parchment paper) on top of two baking sheets. Ready?

Set your microwave to 50 percent power and cook the butterscotch chips and peanut butter mix for 4–5 minutes, stopping to stir it *every minute* until it is completely melted and very hot, but not scorched.

The melted butterscotch mixture will cool and harden quickly, so work fast as you do these next steps. First, with your child's help dump in your "hay" mixture, stirring just a bit to begin to coat the noodles. Then add in your extras (chocolate chips and marshmallows) and stir right away.

Working quickly, use a spoon to drop small mounds of the mixture ("haystacks") onto the wax paper.

Put your cookies into the refrigerator for about 1 hour before eating.

bubble power 45

Use bath time to help your child understand God's total forgiveness.

experience

Before bedtime, invite your child to draw some pictures of what she did during the day, using washable markers. If your child is a very clean artist and doesn't normally get ink on her hands or arms as she colors, sneakily encourage it by having her trace her hands and bare feet on paper. You could also invite your child to draw directly on her palms. The goal here is for your child to get some marker on her skin.

supplies:
- washable markers
- paper
- bath tub and water
- bubble bath
- bath soap or shower gel
- washcloth

Then draw a bath and make it extra bubbly. As your child gets undressed, draw attention to the marker on her skin and hand her a *dry* washcloth to try to wipe it off. (It won't work.) Then invite your child to get into the bubbly tub and use the washcloth and some soap or body wash to scrub those marks away until they completely disappear.

connection

Scripture provides us this amazing picture of God's forgiveness: having our sins washed away. When he was overcome with guilt because of his adultery with Bathsheba and the murder of her husband, David cried out to God, "Wash away all my iniquity and cleanse me from my sin" (Ps. 51:2). Like the powerless dry washcloth, we are unable to remove our own sin. Only God can do it! And this verse captures the very essence of God's forgiveness: Our sins that were once there are washed off and are now gone.

As your child scrubs off the marks on her skin, simply draw her attention to the spiritual picture the act of washing provides for us, saying something like, "Did you know that when we ask Jesus to forgive our sins, it's just like this? It's like he washes them away."

Say, "Remember when we tried to get those marks off with the dry washcloth and it didn't work? That's how it is in real life. We can't get rid of our sin on our own." Then share the words of Psalm 51:2 with your child. Invite your child to picture God washing her sins away, just like the marks on her skin that have completely disappeared. Help your child to get a glimpse of how total and complete God's forgiveness is.

exploration

You may want to ask your child questions like these:

* How does it feel to know that when God forgives you, he *completely* forgives you—he washes your sin away?
* Do you think there are ever any sins that are so bad that God can't forgive them and wash them away?
* How important is it to ask for God's forgiveness when we sin? What effect might it have on us if we don't ask for forgiveness?
* Why does God forgive us?

Have fun eating this healthy snack together, and learn about evangelism in the process!

experience

This snack is super fun for kids to eat as they pretend to "fish" for their food. Create fishing poles by cutting carrots and celery stalks into thin rods. In a small bowl, stir one to two tablespoons of honey into some peanut butter to make it smooth and sweet. Then create your fishing "pond" by filling up another bowl with Goldfish crackers. Toss in a small handful of raisins and about fifteen M&Ms; then mix it up. (If you put in too many M&Ms, that's all your child will try to catch!)

supplies:
- carrots and celery (cut into 4- to 5-inch sticks)
- peanut butter
- honey
- Goldfish crackers
- raisins
- M&Ms
- 2 bowls

Show your child how to fish by dipping the end of a carrot or celery fishing pole into the peanut butter; this is the bait. Next your child can dip his fishing pole into the pond to see what he'll catch. Last, chomp it off the pole and eat it! (Encourage your child to eat the fishing poles too, rather than just licking the snacks off the end.)

connection

Jesus said something remarkable when he was calling his first disciples: "Come, follow me, and I will show you how to fish for people!" (Matt. 4:19 NLT). Fishing was Simon Peter and Andrew's career until Jesus called them to a new focus in life: "catching" people with the good news!

Share this Bible verse with your child and explain to him that Jesus also calls him to "fish for people." Explore together what your child thinks this might mean. Then share in simple terms that God wants him to "catch" people for God by sharing his love and telling others about what it means to have a friendship with Jesus. Invite your child to share the names of friends he wants to show Jesus' love to. You can even spontaneously speak prayers aloud together (with your eyes open) as you eat, talking directly to God as you catch fish. For example, you could say, "God, thanks for Tyler's friend Jacob. Help Tyler to show Jacob how much you love him."

exploration

You may want to ask your child questions like these:

* Imagine you were Simon Peter and Andrew and you heard Jesus say this to you. What would you think? What would you wonder?
* What do you think it means to fish for people?
* Do you think God also calls *you* to fish for people?
* Who do you want to share Jesus' love with?

fruit (of the Spirit) salad

*Make a fruit salad to consider
how the Holy Spirit changes our
attitudes and behaviors.*

experience

Invite your child to help you design and put together a fruit salad consisting of nine types of fruit. You may want to include watermelon, cantaloupe, green grapes, kiwi, oranges (or mandarin oranges), strawberries, blueberries, banana slices, and pineapple chunks (with juice). Other options that taste great include apples, raspberries, honeydew melon, or peaches.

supplies:
- nine different types of fruit
- a sharp knife (for you) and a dull or plastic knife (for your child)
- a melon-baller
- spoons
- nine bowls or containers
- one large serving bowl

Cut each fruit into unique and different shapes, such as melon balls, grape halves, kiwi discs, orange half-wedges, and quartered strawberries. Help your child cut several of the fruits on her own. Put each fruit in its own bowl or container.

Before you add each fruit to the serving bowl, talk about Galatians 5:22–23. Pick a fruit to represent each trait listed in the passage, adding them to the serving bowl one at a time. Add the pineapple (with juice) last; the acidity in the juice will prevent the banana slices from quickly browning. Stir the salad a bit, and then eat it together.

connection

Using actual fruit is a fun way to help your child remember the fruit of the Spirit. Repeat Galatians 5:22–23 and its basic elements several times during this activity to help it really sink in. As you make and eat your salad, talk about what Paul meant by the word *fruit.* Make it simple for your child by asking her to imagine she's a plant or a tree; like a plant, the fruit are the things that naturally grow out of her life. When she has the Holy Spirit in her life, the "fruit" mentioned in this passage will grow for all to see.

As you eat your salad, pick a fruit from it and try to remember with your child which fruit of the Spirit it symbolized. Then brainstorm ways a child can express that fruit. For example, peace can be expressed by choosing not to argue with a sibling. Patience can be expressed by purposefully not complaining when waiting for a snack or a meal. Kindness can be expressed by playing with another child who feels lonely. Invite your child to also help you brainstorm grown-up ways you can demonstrate the fruit of the Spirit. Be sure to take her suggestions seriously—God may challenge you through your child's words!

Wrap up by reading Galatians 5:22–23 one more time, then each picking one fruit of the Spirit you want to focus on expressing that day. Share your commitment with each other; then pray together, asking God's Spirit to help you live it out.

exploration

You may want to ask your child questions like these:

* Which of these fruits of God's Spirit is easiest for you to live out?
* Which is the hardest to live out?
* How does God help us express the fruit of the Spirit?

*Use a backyard soccer game to cast
a spiritual vision for your child.*

experience

If you've ever watched a broadcast of soccer (excuse me, *fútbol)* on Spanish-language television, you've heard the amazing, crowd-thrilling, contagious, and amazingly *long* shout of the announcer when a team scores: *"Goooooooool!"* All the efforts of the team—all the running and sweating and kicking and defensive plays—are all focused in one direction: scoring a goal. And scoring a goal in soccer is rewarding because it takes a lot of work. This is true from professional soccer all the way down to preschool soccer leagues in which kids mob the ball and frantically kick each other in the shins.

supplies:
- soccer ball
- soccer goal
- cones, or other markers

Have some fun playing soccer with your child in the backyard; play one-on-one or take turns practicing shooting goals. Whenever one of you scores a goal, make a big deal celebrating the accomplishment.

connection

Kids don't carry the weight of the world on their shoulders like we grown-ups tend to do. They don't have to pay bills or log in hours or do five loads of laundry or cook dinner or maintain the car or whatever else fills up your to-do list. But it doesn't take long for a child to begin to sense the expectations being placed on him by parents, teachers, and coaches. There are many worthy goals in this life for your child to aim at, like responsibility at home, good behavior, and putting his best effort into music lessons or sports. But there's no higher goal more deserving of his focus than pleasing God.

Use your soccer-playing experience to share this simple yet profound verse with your child from Paul's epistle to the Corinthians: "We make it our goal to please him" (2 Cor. 5:9). Repeat the verse together, trying to memorize it. Talk together about how, in soccer, you focus on that goal the entire time, doing everything you can to get the ball in. Make the connection to the spiritual life by saying something like, "You can make pleasing God your number one goal in life. There are lots of things that are important, but nothing is as important as pleasing God. That's the goal you want to aim for in everything you do."

exploration

You may want to ask your child questions like these:

* How is pleasing God like kicking a ball straight into the goal?
* What things can we do to please God?
* What things take our minds off that important goal?
* What are some ways we can help each other stay focused on the goal of pleasing God?

God rocks! 49

*Commemorate God's faithfulness
by creating stones of remembrance.*

experience

Lay out some newspaper on the ground and ready several colors of paint. Then reflect with your child on ways God has blessed and cared for your family. With an older child, invite her to think about the past year and talk together about a few specific examples of God's work in your family's life. With a younger child, zero in on a much shorter time frame, such as the past week or even the past day. Each of you should think of at least one specific thing God has done or provided, and then paint your rock to represent it in some way. For example, you could paint a word or a letter on your rock, a picture, or just a design that represents the event or example you're thinking of. After the paint has completely dried, coat your rocks with at least one layer of weather-ready sealant (available at craft stores).

supplies:
- large smooth rocks
- weather-resistant acrylic paint
- sealant
- newspaper
- paintbrushes

connection

It's so easy to forget the wonderful things God has done in our lives. The Israelites faced the same temptation to forget, and so when

God did something amazing, God also helped them to remember what he'd done. For example, God directed his people to set up an altar of stones that would help them always remember the miracle he'd done in allowing them to cross the Jordan River on dry ground. Share this amazing account from Scripture with your child, found in Joshua 3:7—4:9.

As you decorate your stones, talk together about what they represent, naming the many ways you want to remember God's faithfulness to you. Then, when the rocks are completely dry, select a spot in your yard where you can place them, such as in a flowerbed or near your front door. Talk together about how you will both try to remember God's faithfulness each time you see the rocks.

exploration

You may want to ask your child questions like these:

* Why do you think God asked the Israelites to set up rocks from the river?
* What are all the ways God cares for us? What are some special things God has done for us?
* What does your rock represent? Why is it important to you to remember that?

it's empty! 50

*Eat a breakfast treat that symbolizes
the story of Christ's resurrection.*

experience

These treats are perfect for Easter but can be
enjoyed any time of the year for breakfast or as a
fun dessert. Resurrection rolls are very easy to
make, so be sure to have your child involved in
every step of the instructions.

supplies:
- ingredients
  (see below)
- kitchen tools

connection

As you follow each step of this recipe, use it to tell the story
of Jesus' resurrection in a lighthearted way. First, as you put the
marshmallows onto the dough, say something like, "This is how
they placed Jesus' body in a tomb after he died on the cross."

Next, as you seal up the "tombs" tightly, remind your child that
Jesus' body was securely sealed inside a tomb. You may also want
to explain to your child that tombs in Jesus' time were a bit like
caves; as they form their dough into round balls, they can picture
the marshmallow inside each little cave.

Here's the magic of this snack: As they bake, the marshmallows
melt away! After you let the rolls cool for a few minutes, give your
child a roll and let him take a bite. Together you can celebrate how

the "tomb" is empty! Emphasize here that on Easter morning when Jesus' friends went to visit the tomb, they found it empty because he had miraculously risen from the dead.

resurrection rolls

ingredients

- 1 can of Pillsbury Grands! biscuits
- jumbo marshmallows
- cinnamon

Preheat the oven to 350 degrees.

Cut jumbo marshmallows in half; you'll need one half for each biscuit.

Flatten each biscuit by pinching it and gently stretching it until it is thin and about 5–6 inches in diameter.

Place a jumbo marshmallow half in the middle of each piece of dough.

Sprinkle some cinnamon on top of each marshmallow.

Next, wrap and fold the dough around each marshmallow so they are securely covered. Pinch all the edges together well to seal it in; each roll should now look relatively like a round ball. (You can roll them and squeeze them to make them more ball-like as needed.)

Place the rolls on an ungreased baking pan, seams down. Bake the rolls for 12–15 minutes.

When they're done, allow the rolls to cool just a bit before eating.

exploration

You may want to ask your child questions like these:

✳ How do you think Jesus' friends felt when he was dead and his body was sealed in a tomb?

✳ What do you think they thought or felt when they discovered the tomb was empty on Easter Sunday? Imagine you were there—what would you have thought or felt?

✳ Why is the miracle of Jesus' resurrection from the dead so important to us?

*Use a simple science experiment to
consider the power of Jesus' healing touch.*

experience

Your child will feel like her touch is magical as
she tries out this fun science experiment. Lay a
clean dinner plate on a flat surface and slowly fill
it with water; let it settle for at least one minute so
that the water's surface is totally calm and smooth.
Next, have your child gently sprinkle talcum powder
(or pepper) over the plate until the surface of the
water is lightly covered by it.

supplies:
• clean dinner plate
• talcum powder
  (or black pepper)
• bar of soap
• cup of water

Have your child dip her pointer finger into a cup of water then
rub it onto a bar of soap until the tip of her finger is pretty soapy.
Prompt your child to slowly dip her finger into the water near one
edge of the plate. Very quickly, the powder (or pepper) will "move" to
the opposite side of the plate.

What looks like magic is basic science: The soap disrupts the water's
surface tension. The stronger area of tension (opposite the soapy
finger) will pull the powder its direction.

connection

It's pretty exciting to feel like you've got a magic touch. Use this experience to point out that Jesus truly *did* have a "magic" touch. He performed amazing miracles, healing diseases with his touch and his words. Invite your child to imagine she was present in the crowd watching as Jesus performed one of the amazing healing miracles recorded in Scripture, such as in Matthew 8:1–4, when Christ healed a man of leprosy. What might it have been like to see the amazing power and love of Jesus' healing touch? If your child is interested, take a quick tour through Matthew 8 and 9 and talk about the many healing stories contained in just these two chapters, including the centurion's servant (8:5–13), Peter's mother (8:14–15), the Gadarenes demoniacs (8:28–34), the paralyzed man (9:2–8), the ruler's daughter (9:18–26), the bleeding woman (9:20–22), the two blind men (9:27–31), and a demon-possessed man (9:32–33).

Jesus still has a healing touch—he has the power to heal physical ailments and to mend broken hearts. If your child has areas in which she needs healing, such as a physical ailment or an emotional hurt, pray together for Jesus' special touch on the situation. As you pray, emphasize your trust in God's plan whether or not he provides direct healing.

exploration

You may want to ask your child questions like these:

* What's the most powerful thing a normal human can do with his or her touch?
* Imagine you lived in Bible times and you were sick; then Jesus touched you and healed you. What would you think? What would you feel?
* Are there any hurts in your life—physical or emotional—that you want Jesus to heal?

Turn lovely leaves into art and discuss what trees can teach us about righteous living.

experience

Visit an outdoor area such as a nearby park and go for a short nature walk. As you meander around, prompt your child to collect tree leaves of different shapes and sizes. Once your child has got a good collection of leaves in his bag, say, "Let's look for the biggest, sturdiest tree around." Evaluate the various trees you've walked by and decide together on which tree is the biggest. Next, look for the most beautiful tree; invite your child to use his own criteria to decide which tree is most beautiful to him.

supplies:
• paper or plastic bag
• paper
• crayons

Take your leaves home with you and spread them out on the table. Then show your child how to make leaf-impression art by arranging the leaves, placing a piece of paper on top, and then gently rubbing various colors of crayons on top. *Voila!* Images of the leaves will appear on the paper!

connection

Make a variety of pictures with the leaves. As you do, talk about what the Bible has to say about trees. First ask, "How are people like trees?" Your child may come up with some pretty silly answers and that's perfectly OK. After all, we often don't think of ourselves as tree-like! Then say something like, "Did you know the Bible compares people to trees? It talks about people who trust God and live rightly as being like growing, vibrant trees."

Read Psalm 1:1–3; Proverbs 11:28; and Jeremiah 17:7–8 to your child and talk about what these passages mean, using the questions below. Remind your child of the big, sturdy tree and the beautiful tree he found and say something like, "When we trust in God and live rightly, our faith grows stronger and sturdier. We grow and thrive. Like a tree grows green leaves, our lives produce good things—people can see that we're spiritually growing."

Write out Proverbs 11:28 on the bottom of one of your child's pieces of leaf art and ask, "How can we 'thrive' like a green leaf? What should we do to grow spiritually like that?" Then affirm your child by pointing out ways you see righteousness, spiritual growth, and trust in God in his life.

exploration

You may want to ask your child questions like these:

* A tree near water grows so well because its deep roots suck up the nourishment it needs. We can grow like that when we're close to God! How can we be close to God?
* What do you think it means to trust in God? What are some small ways we can show our trust in God? What are some big ways we can show our trust in God?
* How can we live in a way that's so vibrant and growing that other people notice?

Help your child develop lifelong habits like Lectio Divina *and contemplative reading.*

experience

When you next read a Bible story to your child, introduce her to one of the ancient methods of scriptural learning described below that combine prayer and meditation with Bible reading.

supplies:
• a children's Bible

Lectio Divina (or "Holy Reading")

This ancient approach to Scripture traditionally has five parts:

(1) *silencio* (quietness and preparation)
(2) *lectio* (slowly reading a Bible passage)
(3) *meditato* (reflection and meditation)
(4) *oratio* (prayer about the passage)
(5) *contemplation* (quiet waiting and prayer)

Your child isn't likely to connect with these Latin terms, so bring this method down to your child's level and do it together in a simple way.

(1) Say something like, "Let's quiet our hearts and minds before we read this story." Allow about five to ten seconds of quietness.

(2) Read the story aloud with emphasis and emotion, perhaps even doing different voices for the various speakers.

(3) Reflect on the passage aloud together by asking, "What do you think this means?" or "What stands out to you about this story? Why?"

(4) Say, "Let's ask God to help us understand more about what this passage means." Then briefly pray aloud, naming your child's ideas she shared in step 3 and asking God for further understanding.

(5) Say, "Let's keep praying but without words now as we listen to God." Allow about thirty seconds (or more if your child is very focused on prayer), then say, "Amen."

Contemplative Reading

In his *Spiritual Exercises*, Ignatius of Loyola outlined a process of contemplative reading. In basic terms, Ignatius encouraged Christians to imagine themselves into gospel stories. Children are experts at this. In fact, they could teach us logic-bound grown-ups a thing or two.

Read a story to your child from one of the four Gospels. Next say, "Let's ask God to help us imagine what it was like for the people in this story." After a short prayer, invite your child to close her eyes, and do the same yourself. Then use prompts like these to bring the account to life in your mind: "What do you think the sounds were? The smells? What might the weather have been like? Imagine the other people nearby—what do they look like? What were they saying or doing?"

Now say something like, "Let's imagine each event in this story." Retell the story, stopping every so often to ask things like, "How do you think Jesus said this? What do you think he sounded like? How do you think the people reacted when they heard him say this?" Your child may answer your prompts aloud or she may simply imagine things quietly; either approach is fine.

Wrap up with prayer, inviting your child to talk to Jesus as a friend.

connection

Studying Scripture is an important skill your child will develop when she gets older. But often we grown-ups focus so much on *intellectual* interactions with Scripture that we neglect the *devotional* approaches to God's Word that seem to come naturally to kids. As you introduce your child to these methods of reading God's Word and practice them regularly together, you're helping to develop lifelong habits in her life; habits of connecting with God's Word not only in terms of facts, but with true intellectual *love*.

exploration

You may want to ask your child questions like these:

- ✻ How did God speak to you in this Bible story or in your prayer and quietness?
- ✻ How do you think God wants you to put this story into action in your own life?

54 pictures of praise

Challenge your child to capture images of Psalm 148 in action.

supplies:
- a digital camera

experience

On a day with fairly good weather, review with your child the basics of how to use your digital camera and then invite him to put his photography skills to work. Give him this assignment: to capture images of things in nature (plants, animals, insects, or inanimate objects) "praising God."

Read Psalm 148 to your child and briefly discuss the idea that all the things in the created world praise God in their own way. Say something like, "Your job now is to try to take pictures of it happening!" (If your child is very literal and is not sure what the passage is speaking of figuratively, connect some dots for him by giving examples of things he could photograph, such as a bug crawling, a plant soaking up sunlight, a cloud floating, a bird singing, or a creek flowing.)

Go to a natural area together, such as your backyard or a nearby park, and keep an eye on your child while he takes pictures. When he's done, look through his images together and talk about the pictures of praise he's captured.

connection

Once you've reviewed your child's photographs together, read Psalm 148 with him again. Use the questions below to explore what this passage means. Then connect his photographs directly to the passage, drawing attention to images of clouds or weather (verses 4 and 8), landscape images or pictures of trees and plants (verse 9), and images of living creatures (verse 10). Say something like, "When we think about praise, we often think of people saying or singing words to God. But everything God made praises him in its own way. Birds sing praises. Plants praise God silently, by growing. Rivers praise God by flowing. And worms praise God by . . . being wormy!"

exploration

You may want to ask your child questions like these:

* How do people praise God? How do animals, plants, or other created things praise God?
* Which photo of praise that you took is your favorite? Why?
* Were you surprised by how much praise was going on around you? Why or why not?
* What are some ways our family can praise God together?

bonus!

Select a particularly striking photograph your child took and have it printed in a 5 x 7 or 8 x 10 format. Mat the picture and write the words of a Bible verse on the mat, such as Psalm 148:13 or 150:6. Then frame the picture and hang it up somewhere in your house for all to see.

55 quite a kingdom

Build a castle together to imagine what heaven will be like.

supplies:
- Legos or wooden building blocks
- other toys

experience

Dedicate fifteen minutes or more to building an elaborate castle with your child using Legos, blocks, or other toys. Engage your imagination as you play, creating courtyards and rooms, a moat and drawbridge, battlements and turrets, stables and gardens. Invite your child to be the architect, dreaming up ideas for making the castle more elaborate.

connection

Once your castle is complete, talk about the kingdom you've created together and engage in pretend play, visiting the various rooms with dolls or toy soldiers or holding a mock battle with an enemy.

When you're done playing, admire the castle you created and say something like, "Did you know God has a kingdom? In the Bible, Jesus called it the kingdom of heaven." Explain that we don't know exactly what heaven will be like, but it may be a bit like the amazing castle you've built. Share John 14:2–3 with your child, in which Jesus said, "In my Father's house are many rooms; if it were not so, I would have told you. I am going there to prepare a place for you. And if I go and prepare a place for you, I will come back and take you to be with me that you also may be where I am." The KJV renders it more extravagantly, saying, "In my Father's house are many *mansions*" (emphasis added). Explain what a mansion is. Then invite your child to imagine the mansion (or room) Jesus is preparing for her in heaven.

exploration

You may want to ask your child questions like these:

* Would you like to live in a castle? If so, what would you want your castle to be like?
* How do you think heaven might be like the kingdom we created? How do you think it might be different?
* How does it make you feel to know Jesus is preparing a special place just for you in the kingdom of heaven?

56 salty special effects

*Use an art project to discover
how a little salt can change everything.*

supplies:
- watercolor paints
- watercolor paper
- paintbrushes
- water
- paper towels
- sea salt (or table salt)

experience

Van Gogh. Michelangelo. O'Keefe. Monet. _____ (insert your child's name here).

If your child is a budding artist—or maybe he just loves to make a creative mess—sit down together to do some watercolor painting. Watercolor is lots of fun on its own. You can show your child how to mix primary colors to create secondary colors; you can get the paper all wet and then make swirly splatters and dots; you can watch colors blend and bleed into fantastic designs.

Now hold on to your horses: Did you know you can also do special effects with watercolor? No computer animation needed—just a bit of salt.

As you create your paintings together and while the watercolor paint is still very wet, sprinkle some salt onto parts of your painting. (Sea salt is best, but table salt can work too.)

Set the paintings aside to dry. Soon the salt will begin to create a speckled, tie-dye-ish effect in the paint. When the masterpiece is completely dry, brush the salt off and admire your child's handiwork. (Be sure to save it for the future when it will be worth millions!)

connection

Jesus told his followers, "You are the salt of the earth" (Matt. 5:13). There are many interpretations of what this metaphor means: that we are to "flavor" the earth, that we are to preserve the earth, and so on. I'll admit Jesus probably didn't have watercolor painting in mind when he said this! But you can still use this unique interaction with salt to help your child dream about what it means for him to live as the salt of the earth.

Start by making at least one regular watercolor painting together. Then say something like, "I want to show you something really cool we can do to a watercolor painting with salt." Work on your next paintings and sprinkle salt on the wet paint; as you do, talk about Jesus' declaration that we are to be the salt of the earth. Discuss what that means (and be sure to explain how salt was used in Jesus' time for preservation of meat, etc.). Then say something like, "Let's wait and see what this salt does to our paintings."

After your paintings have dried, talk together about the amazing effects the salt had on the paint. Say something like, "Look how the salt changed this picture. Look at how it affected the colors." Then prompt your child to think about himself as "salt" in his world. Talk about how his actions and words can change the whole picture at his school, in your family, and in your neighborhood. Explain that God wants us to live in a way that changes the world around us—there should be an obvious "special effect" on others because of our faith and our desire to serve God. Encourage your child to see himself as God does: as a difference-maker in this world.

Write the words of Matthew 5:13 on the bottom of one of the paintings and hang it in a prominent place as a reminder for your family to live as salt of the earth.

exploration

You may want to ask your child questions like these:

❋ What do we use salt for? What does it do?
❋ What do you think Jesus meant when he called his followers "salt"? What might that mean for us today?
❋ What beautiful things did the salt do to our pictures?
❋ How might God want us to have a beautiful effect on the world around us?

*Use a backyard campout to learn
about the incarnation.*

experience

With your child's "help," pitch a tent in your
backyard for a summertime camping experience.
Put sleeping bags, flashlights, books, and teddy
bears inside. If your child is old enough, plan to
sleep outside together as if you're on a real camping

supplies:
- tent
- other camping
  supplies

trip. With a younger child, use the tent for outdoor pretend play
(imagining being in a mountain forest for example), an afternoon
rest time, or for reading stories before bed. In either scenario, you
can replicate other camping experiences too, like grilling hot dogs
or making foil dinners, eating s'mores, and spending extra time
outdoors.

connection

You may not have realized it, but pitching a tent is one of the
most powerful symbols in Scripture. It's found in John 1:14 in this
description of the incarnation: "The Word became flesh and *made
his dwelling* among us" (emphasis added). In the Hebrew it literally
says Jesus "tabernacled" among us—God came to earth and pitched
a tent here with humankind. Our lifestyles and modern homes

don't lend well to our understanding of this verse, but a first-century audience would've immediately understood the miraculous significance of this statement: The God who crafted the heavens had pitched his tent here among us lowly humans in the body and person of Jesus.

Sometime during your play in the tent, talk with your child about how the Bible tells us that God "set up camp" here on earth. Without going overboard into nuanced theology, share the basic concept of the incarnation with your child by reading John 1:14 and explaining that it uses a word that means "tabernacled." Help your child make the connection to Sunday school stories and pictures of God's people living in tents and worshiping at the tabernacle in the Old Testament. Remind your child that the tabernacle was a tent and God's presence was inside it in a special way. Invite her to make any observations about the comparison between Christ and your real experience of being in a tent. Then say something like, "Just like we came out of our house to live in this tent for awhile today, God came to earth to live in a human body. Isn't that awesome?"

exploration

You may want to ask your child questions like these:

* ✳ Imagine you were God and you were all powerful and created the universe. Do you think you'd want to come to earth and live as a human? Why or why not?
* ✳ Why do you think God did that? Why did Jesus live here on earth?
* ✳ Because he was human, Jesus experienced everything we do—even sadness and pain. How can that help you feel closer to God?

sing a new (old) song 58

*Use music to memorize Bible
verses with your child.*

experience

Rote. Dull. Boring. Imperfect. Impossible. Failure.

These are words often associated with the process of memorization. Though memorizing facts, poems, or Scripture verses comes easily to some, for many of us memorization is a huge struggle. Whether it's striving to remember dates in a high school history class or trying to learn one's home address in kindergarten, plain old repetitive approaches to memorization can cause stress and negative feelings.

supplies:

- CD player
- Bible memory CD (see suggestions below) or iPod and computer with iTunes

That's where mnemonic devices come in—those little tricks that lock facts and phrases into our minds so we can actually remember them. And no mnemonic device works better than music.

The Christian music industry has produced some amazing albums for children that use fun, memorable songs to enable children to memorize Scripture . . . without even realizing it! Our family favorites are Steve Green's *Hide 'Em in Your Heart*, volumes 1 and 2. There are lots of other great albums that use Scripture directly or paraphrase Scripture verses, including the Scripture Memory Songs for Kids series by God Prints and the Scripture Memory Songs series from Max Lucado's Hermie and Friends.

Make it a habit to pop in one of these CDs in the car, during playtime, or at bedtime to fill your child's mind with the life-changing words of Holy Scripture.

connection

There are over a hundred references to singing to the Lord in the book of Psalms; and the book itself is composed of poems set to music. God's people have long used music to memorize and meditate on his Word. As your child locks away songs into his mind, he'll be able to call upon those words of Scripture in any situation. Whether it's on the playground or in the schoolroom or after waking from a scary dream, your child (who may not yet know how to read) can sing comforting words of truth. And the added benefit that's been extremely helpful to me: You'll learn the verses too!

exploration

You may want to ask your child questions like these:

* Which of these songs is your favorite? Why?
* Do you have any questions about what the words of this song mean?
* Why is it important to memorize God's Word?
* When has a Bible verse been helpful to you?

bonus!

You can use this same concept to help your child learn important theological truths from the great hymns of the past. Bobbie Wolgemuth and Joni Eareckson Tada have created a series of books called *Hymns for a Kid's Heart*, which tell kids some of the stories behind the great hymns. The best part? Each book includes a CD of the hymns, recorded with kids in mind!

*Use a science experiment to show your
child the principle behind Philippians 4:8.*

experience

It's a familiar experiment that never loses its ability to amaze! In this activity, you'll see how a plant "circulates" water by absorbing it, transporting it up through the xylem (tubes within the plant), and transpiring it into the air via its leaves. As you use colored water, you'll be able to see its progress through the plant and the final, beautiful effect of coloring the plant's leaves or petals.

supplies:
- celery stalks or white carnations
- sharp scissors
- tall clear glasses of water
- various colors of food coloring
- spoon

Begin with celery stalks (with leaves) or white carnation flowers. Fill several glass jars about two-thirds full with water and invite your child to stir in about twenty drops of food coloring in each glass; you want the water's color to be vibrant and dark. Use a different color for each glass so you can compare their effect on your plants.

Next, prepare your celery or carnations by cutting about a half inch off the bottom of the base or stem and immediately putting the plants into the prepared glasses of water. Set them near a sunny window and wait. Check on them several hours later to see if there is a noticeable effect; check again in twenty-four hours. You can continue this experiment for several days as long as you cut the base of the celery or flower stem about once per day.

connection

The celery or carnations will inevitably become colored by the water they are soaking in. Similarly, we're colored by the thoughts, ideas, behaviors, and actions we regularly soak in. That's why the apostle Paul cautioned Christians to intentionally soak up the good stuff—what's true and right and pure—and avoid the bad stuff.

As you begin your experiment, ask your child, "What effect do you think the colored water will have on the celery (or flowers)?" Then later, as you check on your plants and watch the leaves turn colors, explain how the plant is changed by the water it "drinks." Say something like, "Just like a plant, we're affected by the stuff we soak up into our lives." Ask your child first about negative influences: "How do you think it affects us if we're always around other kids who are rude and disobedient?" or "Do you think playing violent video games has an effect on someone's life? Why or why not?" Talk especially about the hurtful effects of thoughts that don't honor God.

Next, transition to the beautiful and positive effects that come from focusing on godly things. Share Philippians 4:8 with your child and explore together how a person can soak up these good things. Brainstorm specific ways the colors of these godly things can be seen in our lives. Say, "One of the very best ways we can soak up the right things in our thought lives is by memorizing Bible verses and thinking about them." If your child is able, work with her to memorize Philippians 4:8 together and say it to each other throughout the week.

exploration

You may want to ask your child questions like these:

* How are we affected by the stuff that surrounds us? By the people we spend time with? By the entertainment we watch or listen to?

* Who do you know who seems to live out Philippians 4:8? What effects can we see in that person's life of focusing on godly things?
* When have you been negatively affected by spending time doing things or listening to things that weren't pure, noble, admirable, or right?
* How do you want to guard against the influence of negative things soaking into your life? How do you want to try to focus more on good, pure, and God-honoring things?

60 star light, star bright

Look at constellations mentioned in Scripture and talk about the power of God displayed in the heavens.

supplies:
- constellation guide
- flashlight
- telescope (optional)

experience

On a clear night, wake your child up from his sleep to cuddle outside on a blanket with you in the backyard for some stargazing. With an older child, use a constellation guide to locate various constellations in the sky. If you're able, try specifically to find the Pleiades (also called the Seven Sisters), the Bears (Ursa Major and Ursa Minor), and Orion. With a younger child, simply try to find the brightest stars or attempt to do the impossible together: count the stars.

connection

There may be no better "book" to teach us about God's omnipotence and omniscience than the sky above us. Even a young child can "read" its message: There is a great and mighty God who made an awesome universe. As you look at the stars together, share Psalm 147:4–5 with your child and talk about the hundreds of thousands of galaxies and stars and planets in the sky. You can glimpse only a tiny bit of all that is out there! Yet God knows and rules them all. If you've looked at specific constellations with your child, tell him that the Bear, Orion, and the Pleiades are mentioned several times in Scripture, such as Job 9:9 and Amos 5:8. God made them all—and as we look at them we're put in our intended place as worshipers in awe of God's might.

Worship God with your child by praying as you look at the stars or simply looking at them in quietness, meditating on God's power and glory.

exploration

You may want to ask your child questions like these:

* Which constellation is easiest to find? Which is hardest?
* Did you know that thousands of years ago in Bible times, people like Job and Amos looked at these exact same stars and constellations? What do you think about that?
* God knows the name of every single star in the universe. How does that truth make you feel?

bonus!

Is the night sky too cloudy? Is it too cold to go outside? Then amaze your child (and sit in amazement yourself) by touring the constellations using Google Sky (google.com/sky). This computerized view of the sky is made up of images from telescopes like Hubble and from orbiting space observatories.

61 the true treasure hunt

Lead your child on a treasure hunt to help her discover how valuable God's wisdom is.

supplies:
- paper
- pen
- a Bible
- your child's favorite snack

experience

When your child is gone, set up a fun treasure hunt around your house using written clues. You can write clues that will lead her to various spots around your house, like these:

To find the missing treasure box, first dig around in your socks.

Rub-a-dub-dub, the next clue is in the tub.

Mirror, mirror, on the wall, what's the greatest treasure of all?

News, blues, lose, choose . . . the next clue's hidden in your _____.

The final treasure should be your child's favorite snack, such as fresh-baked cookies and a glass of milk. Next to the "treasure," place a Bible with a bookmark on Proverbs 2:1–5.

When your child gets home, invite her to go on a treasure hunt and give her the first clue. Follow her on her search, cheering her on and helping if she has questions about the clues. When she finally reaches the treasure, celebrate together. Hooray! Invite her to enjoy the treat while you share with her the truth about an even more important treasure.

connection

As your child eats up her treasure, say, "You did an awesome job following the clues and searching for the treasure! Now let me share with you something the Bible says is worth searching for." Read Proverbs 2:1–5 to your child. Then sum it up in your own words, saying something like, "Wisdom is a treasure we should seek with all our hearts." Talk together about how a person can seek wisdom, and share from your own experience about ways you seek after God and his truth.

exploration

You may want to ask your child questions like these:

* ✳ What would you do if you found a real buried treasure?
* ✳ In terms of material things, what are the greatest treasures in this world? In a spiritual sense, what are the greatest treasures?
* ✳ How is wisdom a treasure? How is knowing God like a treasure?
* ✳ What can we do to seek wisdom like a treasure?

62 truth jar

Use stones and a jar to help your child symbolically store up God's Word.

supplies:

- large glass jar
- small to medium-sized stones
- gold paint
- permanent marker

experience

Gather several small and medium-sized stones; you'll want enough to be able to fill your large glass jar. Paint each stone gold and set it out to dry.

When everything's ready, sit down with your child and show him the jar and stones. Read Psalm 119:11 from the English Standard Version to your child: "I have stored up your word in my heart that I might not sin against you." Say something like, "There are many ways we can store up God's Word in our hearts—by reading it, talking about it, pondering it, praying it, and memorizing it." Explain that you're going to use the jar together to symbolically "store up" God's Word.

Over the next several weeks, whenever your child memorizes a Bible verse, meditates on a passage, or discusses a Bible story with you, give him a stone and invite him to write the reference to the Bible passage on the stone or a word describing its significance. Then invite him to place it in his jar. Stay on top of this commitment by encouraging your child along the way, supporting any significant step he takes to store away God's Word. Keep working on this together until the jar is full!

connection

When the jar is full of stones, celebrate with your child and invite him to empty out the jar, one stone at a time, recalling the various passages, stories, prayers, and discussions he's "stored" away. Invite your child to share any reflections he has on the various stones.

Then talk together about the immeasurable value of storing up God's Word in one's heart and how important it is to form a *habit* of doing so. Tell your child about a Bible verse or story you've stored away in your heart that's been especially meaningful to you. Review again the many ways we can store God's Word in our hearts: memorization, prayer, learning Bible stories, pondering (meditating on) Bible passages, singing Bible verses, study, and more.

exploration

You may want to ask your child questions like these:

* What do you think it means to store up God's Word in your heart?
* What verse or story represented by your stones really stands out to you? Why?
* How has storing up these verses and stories helped you know God more?

63 white (and yummy) as snow

Make and eat snow ice cream together to help your child grasp the fullness of God's grace.

supplies:
- fresh snow
- ingredients (see below)
- kitchen tools

experience

On a cold winter day when a new layer of freshly fallen snow covers the ground, invite your child to help you make a delicious winter treat: snow ice cream! Follow the instructions below or use your own family recipe.

connection

Before you add the liquid mixture to the snow (which will discolor it), draw your child's attention to how white the snow is. Ask, "Would you want to make snow ice cream with dirty, gray snow? Why not?"

Then, as you eat the snow ice cream and look at the fresh white snow outside, share the words of Isaiah 1:18 with your child: "Though your sins are like scarlet, they shall be as white as snow." Say something like, "All of us do wrong things. We do sinful actions. We have sinful thoughts and selfish feelings. None of us is pure and clean inside like that clean, white snow. This verse compares our sins to the color scarlet—deep, dark red. But God's forgiveness changes us inside to be like pure, clean, white snow."

Invite your child to marvel at the power of God's forgiveness and how fully his grace covers our sin. When you finish eating your ice cream, pray a simple prayer together using Isaiah 1:18, something like this: "God, my sins make me dirty. But you forgive me and clean those sins away. Your grace has made me like white, clean snow. Thank you for your grace. Amen."

exploration

You may want to ask your child questions like these:

✳ What is beautiful about fresh snow? How does snow change as it gets dirty?

✳ Why do you think God compared forgiveness to white snow? How does that word picture help you understand God's grace and forgiveness?

snow ice cream

ingredients

- 8–10 c. fresh, clean snow
- 1 14-oz. can sweetened condensed milk
- 1 tsp. vanilla

Help your child use a measuring cup to fill a large mixing bowl with 8–10 full cups of fresh, fluffy snow.

In a separate bowl, stir together the condensed milk and vanilla. If it's not thinned down enough, add 1 tsp. of whole milk and stir it in.

Slowly pour the liquid into the bowl of snow while you gently stir it in. When it's mixed sufficiently, serve it up in bowls with spoons and start eating. Yum!

Loving God with all our heart (emotions), soul (spiritual life), and mind (intellect) has to do mostly with inner thoughts, feelings, and practices. But loving God with all one's strength is where the rubber meets the road—it's where our inner feelings, inner faith, and inner thought life translate into outward expression. It's where we put action, effort, and sometimes even sweat into applying God's Word and living the way he's called us to.

"Love the Lord your God . . . with all your strength."
—Jesus (Mark 12:30)

Without putting strength to our faith—without effort and actions that demonstrate what we believe—our faith is rendered hollow, empty, and meaningless. Consider this challenge from James:

Dear friends, do you think you'll get anywhere in this if you learn all the right words but never do anything? Does merely talking about faith indicate that a person really has it? For instance, you come upon an old friend dressed in rags and half-starved and say, "Good morning, friend! Be clothed in Christ! Be filled with the Holy Spirit!" and walk off without providing so much as a coat or a cup of soup—where does that get you? Isn't it obvious that God-talk without God-acts is outrageous nonsense? (James 2:14–17 MSG)

This section is about enabling our kids in the "God-acts" department—teaching them, helping them, and inspiring them to put some muscle to their love for God and make a difference in the world.

never too young

We protective parents often sell our kids short. In our efforts to protect them from the world's dangers and to keep things "age appropriate," we vastly underestimate their ability to serve God by serving others. Sure, a Habitat for Humanity construction project isn't the place for a clumsy three-year-old to serve God. A homeless shelter for drug users isn't the best environment for a kindergartner. But we need to enlarge our definition of service. There are countless ways young children can put their faith into action—ways that are safe and age appropriate but are also challenging and require a bit of sweat and sacrifice.

Kindness. Teaching our children to be kind is about more than just good manners or getting along with their siblings. We need to help our children see that there's great power in a kind smile, an encouraging word, and a heartfelt hug. Their kind actions can lift up discouraged hearts, heal hurt feelings, spread joy, and help people experience God's love! From crafts to cards to words to body language, the ideas in this section will help your child discover she can change lives by being kind.

Service. We humans don't have to learn self-centeredness. As your kids have shown you, over and over, self-centeredness starts in infancy and sticks with us throughout our lives. We need to be intentional about teaching our kids to combat self-centeredness by choosing to put the needs of others ahead of their own. One powerful way to do this is through practical acts of service, such as helping with household chores, cooking part of the family's dinner, cleaning a classroom at church, or volunteering (with you) in a local community organization. Service can be hard work and it isn't always fun, but by serving together and modeling a God-honoring attitude, you're setting a pattern your child will follow for life.

Giving. We live in a money-obsessed society and it's already targeting your child! Before you know it, our culture will have trained your child on these basics of money management:

(1) Spend tons of money on your own wants.

(2) Spend money you don't even have on more of your own wants.

(3) Look for happiness in your accumulated pile of stuff (and if you haven't found it yet, just keep spending . . . you will!).

(4) If you have money left over (which you never will), assuage your guilty conscience by periodically giving the financial scraps to a good cause.

This is about as contrary to biblical teaching as possible. Though your child may not have much money now, don't wait until the teen years to try to teach her about money. Instead, use a variety of approaches to train your child in wise stewardship and generous giving. The actions your child learns to take to honor God with her money will stand in stark contrast with the world around her and will help her faith shine for all to see.

pint-sized mission field

God can use your child to change her world, and it's your job to show her *how*. Through the ideas in this section and "God-acts" ideas of your own, you can help your child to see her words, her choices, her behavior, and her acts of service as signposts that declare her love for God and point others his way.

64 big-time service

Assist your child in serving the family by doing a "big person" chore around the house.

supplies:
- cleaning supplies

experience

I was pretty surprised the other day when my five-year-old asked to have "brush your teeth" removed from his list of chores and wanted it to be replaced with "set the table."

"That's not a real job," he told me as he pointed to the picture of a toothbrush. "Setting the table is a *real* job, Mom."

His request reminded me of how important it is that acts of service and responsibilities feel *meaningful* to a child. Give your child an opportunity to do a significant act of service by performing a grown-up chore. Make it a real household job that you or your spouse normally do, such as vacuuming, mopping, dusting, or sorting laundry. Whatever you select, it should be a job that is outside your child's normal responsibilities and that will feel "grown up" to your child.

Don't force this chore onto your child; rather, present it as a special way to serve God by doing something that really is important for the family. Allow your child to *choose* to do the job; then help her get started and encourage her along the way.

connection

Teaching your child responsibility through chores is an important job for parents. But in this case, your focus should be on providing your child with an opportunity to feel she has *served God* by helping out the family. Share this concept from Ephesians 6:7 with your child: "Work with enthusiasm, as though you were working for the Lord rather than for people" (NLT). While she works (even if she does a less-than-perfect job), encourage her by saying things like "God is so pleased with the way you're helping our family right now."

exploration

You may want to ask your child questions like these:

* How did you just help out the family? Why was that job important?
* Why do you think God wants us to help and serve others?
* Do you know that what you just did is a way to worship God? Have you ever thought of chores that way?

65 crystal-clear evidence

*Make salt crystals with your child
to solidify the importance of outward
actions that reveal inner faith.*

supplies:

- shallow glass or plastic bowls
- one or two charcoal briquettes
- Vaseline
- salt
- ammonia
- Mrs. Stewart's liquid bluing
- water
- spoon
- measuring spoons
- glass pitcher or mixing bowl
- food coloring
- electric fan (optional)

experience

Get ready to feel like a pair of mad scientists as you and your child grow a colorful salt-crystal garden. If your child has never made salt crystals before, don't tell him what to expect; let him be surprised by what takes shape in the bowl over the next few days!

connection

A charcoal briquette with salt sprinkled on it would produce . . . well, nothing. But add a magic solution to the mix and watch what happens. That extra ingredient changes everything!

Theologians have debated for centuries over what the book of James says about the relationship between faith and works. But this experiment boils James's message down into simple and clear terms that aren't up for debate: A person who has true faith in his life *will* exhibit obvious and clear evidence of that faith in his actions.

growing a crystal garden

Note: This experiment uses household ammonia, so it must be done with direct adult supervision and should be stored in an area where your child cannot reach it. If swallowed in large amounts, household ammonia can be toxic. An adult should do all parts of the experiment related to the mixing and pouring of the liquid.

. . . .

Follow these steps together:
1. Prepare your materials. Thoroughly wash and dry a shallow glass or plastic bowl. Then, with your child's help, coat the inside of the bowl with Vaseline. Set 1 or 2 charcoal briquettes in the middle of the bowl.
2. (Adult) Mix the following ingredients together, stirring until the salt dissolves:

- 4 tbsp. Mrs. Stewart's liquid bluing (available at stores or online at www.mrsstewart.com)
- 4 tbsp. household ammonia
- 4 tbsp. water
- 4 tbsp. table salt

3. (Adult) Pour the liquid mixture onto the charcoal.
4. (Child) Squirt a few drops of various colors of food coloring directly onto different areas of the charcoal.
5. (Child) Sprinkle about 1 tbsp. of salt on top of the charcoal.
6. Set the bowl in an area where it won't be disturbed and where your child cannot touch it. (If you're able, set up a small electric fan at a very low speed near the experiment to gently circulate the air. This will aid in the evaporation that causes the crystal growth.)
7. Maintain the experiment by *very* gently sprinkling the charcoal and growing crystals with a pinch of salt after 24 hours and again after 48 hours.
8. (Adult) On the third day of the experiment, mix together another batch of bluing, water, ammonia, and salt, and gently spoon it into the bowl, being careful not to pour it directly onto the growing crystals.
Over the next several days, beautiful, colorful crystals will form, grow, and blossom like a garden. The crystals are very fragile and will fall apart if touched, so be gentle! Allow the experiment to continue for about 3–7 days, checking it often.

When you first begin the experiment, talk with your child about how the bowl can symbolize a person's life. As you pour the special liquid in the bowl, prompt your child to imagine that it's like adding faith to a person's life. As time passes and the salt crystals form, say something like, "We know this bowl has the special liquid ingredients in it because of the evidence that's growing for us to see."

At the end of the week, talk again briefly about this idea: Just like the crystals are physical, visible evidence of the liquid that was added to the bowl, in our lives our actions and words serve as physical and visible evidence of our faith in Christ. Share James 2:14–18 with your child and talk together about how your child can show evidence of his faith by what he does.

exploration

You may want to ask your child questions like these:

* Think of someone you know who really loves Jesus and has faith in him. What is some of the "evidence" of faith we can see in that person's life?
* What are some ways kids can show their faith in Jesus through actions?
* What's one way you want to show evidence of your faith today?

divine valentines **66**

Create "valentines" from God to
encourage leaders in your church.

experience

With your child, identify various leaders in your church who touch your child's life, such as her Sunday school teachers, the children's ministry pastor, the preaching pastor, and the church secretary who helps run the church office. Then say something like, "Let's show each of these people how much God loves them!"

supplies:
- red or pink construction paper
- child-safe scissors
- markers
- other craft supplies like glitter, glue, stickers, or doilies (optional)
- envelopes and postage stamps

Show your child how to cut out large heart shapes by folding a piece of paper in half and then cutting out an ice cream cone shape along the folded edge.

Help your child write:

(front) "God is love" (1 John 4:16).
(back) God loves YOU!

Use craft supplies to decorate the cards like special valentines. Then, when the cards are done, pray by name for each person who

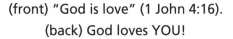

will receive one, asking God to help them feel especially loved by him when they receive their card.

Put the cards in envelopes, address them, and mail them *without* a return address.

connection

Pastors, church administrators, and volunteers like children's ministry workers can go weeks or even months without hearing a genuine thank-you for their efforts. Those who lead us—and who lead our children—need and deserve our thanks, love, and prayers. This simple activity is just one way you can help your child develop the habit of praying for the leaders of your church and showing them love and appreciation.

exploration

You may want to ask your child questions like these:

* How has _____ (pastor's or teacher's name) shown you God's love?
* How has God used _____ (pastor's or teacher's name) to teach you something about the Bible or how to live?
* Why do you think these leaders teach your Sunday school class (or other role)? What may be difficult about their job at church?
* What should we ask God for as we pray for these leaders in our church?

bonus!

Have fun tying this activity in to your regular Valentine's Day routine. Or plan to do this each year during October, which is "Clergy Appreciation Month."

*Take your child along for an afternoon
or evening of volunteer work.*

experience

If your child is in kindergarten or older, invite him to go on a date with you—a special kind of date. It's a "do-good" date, and it will be a time for you to work together to serve God by doing good in the world.

supplies:
• none

Research organizations where you and your child can volunteer together. Consider ideas such as:

* Serve a meal at a Ronald McDonald House (see www.rmhc.com).
* Volunteer with Habitat for Humanity (discover how kids can get involved at www.habitat.org/youthprograms).
* Clean or organize donations at a Christian crisis pregnancy center.
* Read stories to kids at a children's hospital.
* Play games with children at a family shelter.
* Clean up a trail at a local park or nature preserve.
* Volunteer at church (cleaning up rooms, folding bulletins, etc.).

Once you settle on a plan for volunteering, get to it! End the evening with ice cream or another special treat.

connection

Working side-by-side with you to serve others will be a memory your child will always treasure. And your actions will far outstrip any words you say about the importance of helping others. After you serve together, affirm your child for his efforts (even if he complained a bit!) and tell him how pleased God is with his service. If you can, take a picture of the two of you together and print a copy to post in your child's room to remind him of the work you did together.

exploration

You may want to ask your child questions like these:

* ✳ How did you feel as we worked? What did you like about it? What was hard?
* ✳ What did we learn about God during this experience?
* ✳ What are some other ideas you have for ways we can help others together?

get one, give one **68**

*Practice simplicity by donating
toys after birthdays and holidays.*

experience

Select a local nonprofit organization that
accepts donations of used toys or clothes (such as
a homeless shelter, a domestic violence shelter, or
a ministry to low-income moms). Then, a couple of
days after a holiday, sit down with your child and say

supplies:
• none

something like, "Now that we have some new toys (or clothes or books),
we can give away some of our other toys to kids who don't have any."

With your child as an active participant, go through your closet
or bookshelves first and select a few items you'll give away to
those in need. Then move to your child's room and sort through
your child's toys together. Gently and patiently help her decide on
a few items she can part with. To help fight toy accumulation, you
can aim for a one-to-one ratio of new toys to donations, but it
doesn't need to be exact.

connection

Materialism and consumerism are rampant in our society.
Advertisements, friends, and our own selfish natures all shout,
"Me, me, me! I need more for me!" But the reality is that things

don't truly satisfy our inner longings; only Christ does. And Jesus challenged his followers to live counterculturally when it came to material possessions. They were to give radically and generously to the poor rather than accumulating earthly treasures. The Get One, Give One principle is just one small way your family can live counterculturally.

Get One, Give One is a practice that can become a natural habit; you can do it regularly together to help keep your focus on giving rather than keeping. After all, what kid really needs 250 toys accumulated over a few years? Meanwhile, that little boy living in a domestic violence shelter with his mom would probably really love that bag of slightly used Matchbox cars!

As you form the Get One, Give One habit, reinforce its two-pronged emphasis with your child by saying things like, "We like all this stuff, but we really don't need all this stuff. Stuff doesn't make us happy; only Jesus can make us truly happy." Or "I'm so proud of you for choosing to give that teddy bear away. The child who receives it, who probably doesn't have many toys, will love it very much."

exploration

You may want to ask your child questions like these:

* What difference will it make in the life of a needy child to give him these toys?
* What difference will it make in your life to give away some of these possessions rather than having so many things?
* Why do you think it is important for us to try to live simply rather than to just get more and more stuff for ourselves?
* What's tough about giving possessions away? What do you like about giving things away?

bonus!

David Shannon, one of my kids' favorite authors and illustrators, has a great book called *Too Many Toys*. In this story, a young boy who's swimming in toys is challenged to give some away. I won't spoil the charming ending of the story, but suffice it to say that it'd be a great book to read when you and your child pack up your own cardboard box with toys to donate!

69 giveaway garden

Help your child plant a flower patch with a purpose.

supplies:
- flower seeds
- shovel
- soil
- flower pots (optional)
- scissors
- ribbon
- plastic disposable cups or sandwich bags
- paper towels

experience

In the late spring, transform a corner of your yard into a Giveaway Garden for your child. Dig away dirt and weeds, mix in some good quality potting soil, then get started. Tell your child you're going to grow flowers together that you'll use to encourage other people. Bring your child along to the store to select two to four different floral seed packets. (You may want to focus on easy-to-grow varieties like cosmos, bachelor buttons, marigolds, and zinnias.) Spend a morning planting your flower seeds together, and read the seed packet instructions about how to care for the plants as they grow.

Once the plants start blooming, take time every few days to help your child snip off some fresh flowers to give away to someone. Tie the flowers together with a ribbon; then bundle up the flower stems in damp paper towels and stick the ends into a cup or paper bag.

Help your child think through all the different people he could encourage by giving them a surprise bouquet: a neighborhood playmate, his Sunday school teacher, his teacher, an elderly person in your neighborhood, his sibling, officers at the police station or fire station (you could drive him there), and so on. Talk about how your child's gift of flowers will bring joy and happiness to someone's day. When he's ready, send your child off to deliver the flowers (while you watch from a distance). If he's not sure what to say, suggest something simple like, "These are from our garden. I thought you might like them."

connection

Encouraging words can go a long way to lift a person's spirits, but a surprise bouquet from a bright-eyed child? That's like an encouragement extravaganza! When your child sees the power of his surprise bouquet—when he watches a grown-up's face break into a smile of genuine delight and surprise—he'll realize he's done something really significant! With a little help from you reminding him to check the garden, snipping flowers to give them away will become addictive!

As your child prepares a bouquet to give away and once he's decided who he'll give it to, say something like, "You are going to bring so much joy to _____'s day! I'm proud of you for showing Jesus' love in this way." Invite your child to pray with you for the person who will receive the flowers, asking God to fill him with hope and joy and peace.

exploration

You may want to ask your child questions like these:

* How do you think _____ will feel when you surprise him with these flowers?
* What do you like about giving away flowers?
* How do you think your new habit of encouraging people with flowers is affecting them? How is it affecting you?

70 glow-stick tag

*Turn a twilight game into
a picture of missional living.*

supplies:

- new glow
  sticks (two
  per person)
- glow necklaces
  and bracelets
  (optional;
  glow-in-the-
  dark products
  like these are
  available at
  most party
  supply stores)

experience

In the autumn or early spring when night falls early, bundle up your family for a fun game of glow-stick tag in your backyard. You'll want to play this game around twilight, when it's sufficiently dark (so the light from the glow-sticks really shine) but when there's still enough light for people to see where they're going. (Running smack dab into a tree will ruin the fun!)

First, get ready to play by "turning on" each glow stick (follow the directions on the packaging). Give every player two glow sticks and, if you've got glow necklaces, have every player put some on as headbands, wristbands, and anklets.

The rules are simple: Every player must hold a glow stick in each hand throughout the entire game. The sticks cannot be hidden in pockets—they must be in full view. Then you simply play tag! One person is "It" and the others run and hide in various places in your playing area. "It" needs to try to tag another player by touching him or her with "Its" glow stick. Once someone is tagged by "Its" glow stick, that person becomes "It" and the game continues.

connection

After the game, talk together about how much fun you had. Then share Matthew 5:14–16 with your child and use the questions below to help your child think about how she can let her "good deeds shine out for all to see" (NLT). Invite your child to think about how this world is "dark" for people who don't know Christ. Encourage her to envision how her life can shine brightly in that darkness; how, like in the game, others will be able to see her clearly as she "glows" with Christ's love.

Bring the focus in on Matthew 5:16, which makes a strong connection between "good deeds" and a shining light. We don't shine simply by having a personal faith that's kept private. We don't put our light under a bowl—or put our glow stick in our pocket! In other words, faith isn't a private matter. It's something bright and obvious to everyone because it is integrated into how we live. Brainstorm with your child various ways God desires that she "glow" for Jesus. How can she be a light through her words, actions, and attitudes? Might God want her to talk about Jesus with others? Are there ways she can serve or help others? How could happiness, joy, patience, and compassion shine out of her in her everyday life and interactions with others?

Don't end the learning process with discussion; move one step deeper by each sharing a commitment about a specific way you'll shine your light tomorrow through good deeds.

exploration

You may want to ask your child questions like these:

✳ How is this world "dark" for people who don't know Jesus? What feelings, experiences, or tough situations are like darkness for people?

* What do you think it means for Jesus to call you the "light of the world"?
* How might we be tempted to hide our light?
* What kinds of "good deeds" shine the light of Jesus for others to see (Matt. 5:16)? What are some ways a kid like you can shine and glow with the light of Jesus?

grooming generosity **71**

*In a world of selfish spenders, train
your child to think of others first.*

experience

Tithing is an important principle from the
Bible that's particularly emphasized in the Old
Testament; it's the idea of giving the first tenth of
one's harvest or income to God. In the New
Testament, the stakes are raised even higher as
Jesus emphasizes radical, sacrificial giving (see
Matt. 5:42; Mark 12:41–44).

supplies:
- three or four
  empty coffee cans
  with lids
- paper
- glue or tape
- markers
- stickers
- other craft supplies

Christian speaker and author Nathan Dungan
has created an organization called Share Save
Spend (www.sharesavespend.com), and its basic mission is to teach
young people sound financial principles. Dungan suggests giving kids
an allowance that's easily divisible by three. Each time you distribute
the allowance, lead your child in prioritizing his money by *first* putting
one-third into a "Share" bank, and *second* putting one-third into
a "Save" bank, and only *last* putting the final third into a "Spend"
bank. Dungan intends for children to use their Share money for church
offerings as well as for other opportunities to give to those in need.

Our family has altered this idea a bit by creating four bank
containers labeled "God," "People," "Save," and "Self" and by making

our oldest son's allowance easily divisible by four. We've done so to make it clear that a portion always goes to church, while also enabling our son to save money to give to people in need.

Use coffee cans wrapped in paper to create "piggy banks" with your child for his allowance. Label one "Share," one "Save," and one "Spend" (or "God," "People," "Save," and "Self"). Help your child decorate them any way he'd like; cut a slit in the lid of each new bank so your child can slip money into it. When the banks are done, line them up in order and begin the weekly practice of distributing the allowance into each container.

connection

Your family, like many, may give to your church according to the system of tithing: giving a full 10 percent off the top of your paycheck. And if you're like most people, it's likely that the other 90 percent is spent mostly on needs (like bills and groceries). In other words, you don't spend the other 90 percent on toys for yourself! Herein lies the problem with using tithing (a 10 percent approach) with a child to teach him how to give to God. Since he doesn't spend the rest on needs, it ends up becoming a scenario in which God gets a pittance of his coins, while a huge percentage (likely 90 percent) goes to ME, ME, ME!

When you use prioritized categories to help your child share, save, and spend his money, you're helping him push back against the dominant message of our culture, which claims that money exists primarily to spend on our own wants! You're helping him put God and others before himself each time he puts the coins in the cans in the proper order. You're also training your child to be a generous giver. You're helping him consistently give a significant amount (not just a pittance in your child's eyes) to the Lord. When he's grown up and advertisements call him to think "ME, ME, ME!" with his money, he'll be equipped to live counterculturally as he regularly gives cheerfully and generously to others.

exploration

You may want to ask your child questions like these:

✳ How do you want to share your money? What ideas do you
have for ways you can help other people with your money?
✳ Why do you think it's important to give to God first?
✳ What do you hope to buy with your "Spend" money?

bonus!

I first learned about Nathan Dungan when I heard his compelling
interview on National Public Radio's show "Speaking of Faith." I
highly recommend listening to the interview. It can be found at
http://speakingoffaith.publicradio.org/programs/moneymorals.

72 more than pen pals

*Sponsor a needy child and facilitate
the start of an overseas friendship.*

supplies:
- paper
- pens
- crayons
- envelopes
- postage

experience

Contact an organization such as World Vision (www.worldvision.org) or Compassion International (www.compassion.com) and sign up to sponsor a child. This monthly commitment of thirty to forty dollars provides a child in a third world country with education and food and also contributes to community projects such as water purification and improvements in agricultural practices. If you're able, involve your child in selecting who you'll sponsor; aim to select a child who is the same gender and age as your own child.

The organization will send you pictures and information about how to keep in contact with your sponsored child. Make a commitment to set aside time once a month to sit down with your child and create correspondence to send to your sponsored child, such as drawings, coloring book pages, letters dictated by your child and written down by you, or your child's own attempts at writing a letter. As you finish each letter, seal it, address it, and then have your child hold it as you say a short prayer together for your sponsored child.

connection

Developing a friendship with a needy child overseas will open your own child's eyes from an early age to see God's call on us to be globally minded Christians. Explain why you are sponsoring the child and tell your child about ways your sponsored child's life is probably very different than your own. For example, you may want to explain that your sponsored child's family likely doesn't have a car or that they may all be living in one very small room with a dirt floor. Describe poverty using examples your child will really understand as you let her know that your family gives money each month to help out.

As you emphasize the differences in your living conditions, also be sure to focus on the similarities between your child and your sponsored child. As she begins to feel a kinship with her new friend overseas, an authentic sense of empathy will develop. Poverty is a weighty issue for all of us, and it can feel especially heavy on a young child's shoulders as she first begins to understand how terrible this problem is in our world. If your child begins to feel sad, discouraged, or confused as you discuss your sponsored child's poverty, *don't* try to gloss over that sadness and make your child feel happy. Instead, thank God for your child's developing compassion for others and affirm that sense of sadness or frustration by telling your child that God hates poverty, that he loves the poor, and that he calls us to do what we can to help those in need. Share a passage such as Psalm 140:12 with your child and thank her for expressing God's love to your sponsored child through prayers and letters.

exploration

You may want to ask your child questions like these:

* What do you think life is like in _____ (sponsored child's) village or country?
* How are you and _____ (sponsored child) similar? What do you have in common?
* How should we pray for _____ (sponsored child)?

73 the one-buck-giveaway challenge

Turn a donation into a family game and help others in the process!

supplies:
- dollar bills

experience

Give each member of your family a dollar bill and pile into the family car together. Say something like "Everybody has a dollar. Our goal is to give away each dollar to help someone in need."

Take a few minutes to brainstorm in the car together; if your child needs help with ideas, mention things like the following:

* Dropping it off at church.
* Purchasing one or two cans of food and delivering them to a food pantry.
* Giving it directly to a homeless person.
* Donating it at a Salvation Army bell-ringing station (Christmas season).
* Buying a candy bar and giving it to a child, neighbor, teacher, or pastor.
* Taking part in a fundraiser (March of Dimes, etc.).

Aim to develop giving ideas within your community—you'll open your child's eyes to the needs around him. Once you've zeroed in on how you'll each give away your dollar, go together to accomplish each mission and cheer each other on in the process.

connection

The problems in this world are big, and many of them require a great deal of money and work to "solve" (if that's possible!). So it's pretty easy to feel like people with lots of money should be doing the work—and people without lots of extra cash shouldn't feel obligated to do anything.

Simply put, that's a lie. Even a dollar given away by a child can make a powerful difference. A small amount—given generously, sacrificially, and sincerely—is counted as riches in the kingdom of heaven. Consider the powerful message Jesus had for the disciples in Mark 12:41–44. He drew their attention to a poor widow who gave only two coins, but he told them her offering was greater than all the others because she gave all she had to live on. Wow! What a convicting message for us grown-ups and for our kids!

As you drive, share the story from Mark 12 with your child and help him think through the thrust of Jesus' message. Then say something like, "A dollar doesn't seem like much in our world, but when we give it to help others its worth can't even be calculated!"

After you give away each dollar, pray together, offering the money to God and asking him to use it to make a difference in the world.

exploration

You may want to ask your child questions like these:

* ✳ How can we make a real difference with a dollar? What are some ways we could help needy people or encourage others with this dollar? Let's brainstorm together.
* ✳ In the story of the widow, what do you think Jesus meant when he said she gave more than everyone else?
* ✳ How do you think Jesus might want you to give money, effort, or time to help others?

74 pass the peas . . . and pray for the world

Create placemats together to guide your family's dinnertime prayers.

supplies:

- large colorful pieces of poster board
- a map of the world that can be cut apart (or images of a global map)
- scissors
- glue sticks
- pens
- stickers
- glitter
- clear contact paper
- *National Geographic* and other magazines (optional)
- *Operation World* by Patrick Johnstone and Jason Mandryk (optional)

experience

Invite your child to help you create globally focused placemats for your family dinner table. Aim to make at least twice as many placemats as you have family members; this will enable you to rotate through the placemats at various dinnertimes. Each placemat should focus on a distinct part of the world, such as a country, region, or continent. Follow these simple steps with your child to make your placemats:

(1) Cut the poster board into large rectangles the size of placemats.

(2) Cut out maps that represent the various countries, regions, or continents you want to feature on the different placemats.

(3) Glue the maps to the placemats and decorate the placemats together with images from magazines that represent the country, with words (such as "Pray for Russia" or "God loves the people of Africa") and with fun drawings and stickers. Talk to

your child about each region's geography, exports, agriculture, wildlife, and culture to help her brainstorm ideas for things to write and draw.

(4) If you have a copy of *Operation World*, write some of the facts and prayer needs about a given region on its placemat.

(5) When everything is dry, use sheets of clear contact paper to "laminate" the placemats on the front and back.

connection

Your child may be too young to go on mission trips, but she certainly isn't too little to become a globally minded Christian. When the placemats you've made are ready, use them to set the table for family dinner. Spend time as you eat talking about the areas represented on the various placemats. Then conclude your meal with prayer for the people living in those regions. Pray specifically for people there who don't know Jesus and for missionaries who may be in those parts of the world shining the light of Christ.

After your meal, put the placemats away for about a week. Then surprise the family by using them again, being sure to mix in some new placemats that weren't used last time. Keep up this pattern of occasionally setting the table with these prayer placemats. Your child will be proud of her handiwork and will develop a global mind-set in the process.

exploration

You may want to ask your child questions like these:

* Which of these regions of the world would you most like to live in? Which of these regions would you least like to live in? Why?
* What do you think life is like for a child your age in that country? What needs do you think people have in that country? In what ways do you think God may want people like us to try to help with those needs?

✳ How would you like our family to pray for the country on your placemat?

bonus!

The authors of *Operation World* have a Web site you could use with an elementary-school age child to pray regularly for people groups around the world. Check out www.operationworld.org and click on "Pray Today" for information about a country you can pray for together.

plaid and polka-dots?

*Let your child pick out his own outfit—
and one for you—and use the clothing to
help him think about the behaviors he
"wears" each day.*

experience

Invite your child to select his clothing for the day, anything from a firefighter costume to a swim suit to pajamas! Compliment whatever he selects. Now here's the gutsy part: Invite your child to select an outfit for *you* to wear too . . . and wear it the whole day!

supplies:
• none

connection

Colossians 3:12 provides a powerful, challenging word picture for us about how our outward actions and behaviors demonstrate our inner faith. Paul wrote, "Therefore, as God's chosen people, holy and dearly loved, clothe yourselves with compassion, kindness, humility, gentleness and patience." *The Message* puts it nicely, saying, "Dress in the wardrobe God picked out for you."

As you put on the clothing, say something like, "Thank you for picking out these clothes for me to wear." Share Colossians 3:12 with your child and say, "Did you know that our attitudes and actions are like clothes? Other people see them, just like they see our clothes. And we can choose, with God's help, to live and act in the 'outfit' he wants us to wear."

Talk about each of the traits Paul points out, inviting your child to share what he thinks compassion, kindness, humility, gentleness, and patience actually *look like* in terms of behavior. Share some examples in adult terms too, talking about specific ways you'll aim to "wear" those traits today. For example, you might say, "I'm going to ask God to help me speak kindly, with love and joy, to each person I talk to today. How do *you* want to show kindness to others today?"

exploration

You may want to ask your child questions like these:

* What's your favorite part of your outfit? What's your favorite part of the outfit you picked out for me?
* How are attitudes and actions a bit like clothing we wear?
* Which piece of clothing from Colossians 3:12 is toughest to "wear"? Compassion, kindness, humility, gentleness, or patience? What makes it tough?
* How do you most want to show your love for God by your actions today?

reduce, reuse, recycle 76

*Turn an environmentalist mantra
into a family stewardship focus.*

experience

You've heard of the three Rs: Reading, (w)Riting, and (a)Rithmetic.

But have you heard of the environmental three Rs? They're Reduce, Reuse, and Recycle. And these three concepts are great avenues for teaching your child to care for God's creation.

If your child hasn't heard it already, introduce your child to the great song "The 3 Rs" by Jack Johnson from the soundtrack of *Curious George*. Sing it together and play it in your house often. Not only is it lots of fun, but it imparts great principles of environmental stewardship to kids at an early age.

supplies:
- CD player or MP3 player
- *Sing-A-Longs and Lullabies for the Film Curious George* CD by Jack Johnson, or MP3 download of the song "The 3 Rs"
- cardboard box or plastic bin (optional)
- paints (optional)

Next, take some time to talk about the three Rs with your child. First, brainstorm ideas for how your family can *reduce* waste, such as using cloth shopping bags rather than plastic, buying durable rather than disposable goods, or composting (see Moment 5 for directions on how to compost). Next, talk about how you can *reuse* the things you have rather than throw them away. For example, you could wear hand-me-down clothing, donate items you don't use anymore, or repair broken items rather than discard them. Last, start a *recycling* bin for your family's trash. If you want, decorate it with your child by painting pictures of the items that can go in it, such as soda cans, newspapers, other paper, plastic bottles, and so on. Commit to model stewardship by making recycling a regular habit for your family.

connection

If your child received a special or expensive Christmas gift, then abused it, neglected it, and trashed it, you'd be appalled . . . and your child would be in *big* trouble! Why? Because it's common sense. We express gratefulness by taking care of the gifts we've been given.

Environmentalism didn't start with recent science—it started in Genesis! God gave Adam and Eve the responsibility of caring for the earth and being its stewards (Gen. 1:26–28; 2:15). And just like we expect our children to care for nice gifts they receive, we too should take great care of the amazing, miraculous, awesome "gift" of creation God has given to us.

Caring for creation is not just a matter of attempting to prevent some looming, nebulous environmental disaster; rather, it's an act of worship and thanksgiving to our Creator. It is one way, among many others, that we show gratefulness to God for all he has done for us and all he has given to us. So as you sing "The 3 Rs," as you talk about them, and as you recycle your trash, emphasize the underlying reason for your actions: gratitude to earth's Maker.

exploration

You may want to ask your child questions like these:

* What are some ways our family can do a better job of reducing waste?
* What ideas do you have of things we can reuse?

✳ What are your favorite parts of God's creation? What do you love about this world God made?

bonus!

Check out some of these Web sites for practical ways to implement the three Rs:

The National Institute of Environmental Health Sciences kids' page: http://kids.niehs.nih.gov/recycle.htm.

The Environmental Protection Agency's "recycle city," an interactive site for kids: http://www.epa.gov/recyclecity.

Creation Care, an evangelical organization committed to environmental stewardship: http://www.creationcare.org.

77 send a shoebox

Get your child involved in putting together a shoebox full of gifts to send to someone in need.

supplies:
- empty shoebox
- wrapping paper
- money to purchase supplies
- donation to Samaritan's Purse

experience

Operation Christmas Child is an initiative spearheaded by Samaritan's Purse, which has delivered more than sixty-one million shoeboxes filled with school supplies, toiletries, toys, and love to needy children around the world. Be a part of this initiative by putting together a shoebox with your child. Join in the program at your church or participate on your own; you can find information online at www.samaritanspurse.org.

With your child's help, purchase supplies for a kid your child's age and gender. Samaritan's Purse recommends filling your shoebox with items such as toys, school supplies, hygiene items, and small clothing items. When you've purchased the materials together, wrap your shoebox and lid, and then fill it up with the goodies! Include something personal like a photograph of your family, a picture colored by your child, or a letter from your child with a self-addressed envelope. Be sure to also include a financial donation in your box, which helps pay the costs of transporting it.

connection

In late fall, the Christmas decorations appear in stores and, if your child is like most, he'll soon be thinking about what he wants for Christmas. Doing a family service project like this one, early on in the Christmas season, is a powerful way to help your child think of people in need rather than buying into our culture's dangerous message of consumerism.

As you put the box together, talk about poverty and encourage your child by imagining together how special and loved the child who receives your package will feel. Then when you're done, put the lid on the box and invite your child to put his hands on the box with you. Pray together for the child who will open the box, asking God to bless that child with love and happiness and peace this Christmas season. Most importantly, pray that the child will discover the love of Jesus when he or she receives the shoebox.

exploration

You may want to ask your child questions like these:

* Imagine what it would be like to live in poverty. What do you think would be the hardest part about living that way? Why?
* What do you think the boy or girl who receives this box will feel when he or she opens it? What do you think he or she will be most excited about?
* In addition to this shoebox, what are some other things our family can do to help people who live in poverty?

78 simon says

*Have a goofy time together helping
your child understand the importance
of honoring God by obeying his parents.*

supplies:
• none

experience

Play several rounds of Simon Says together. Choose one player to be "Simon"; Simon's job is to give the other players commands. When Simon gives a command that begins with the phrase "Simon says," the other players must do exactly what Simon has directed.

Simon can give lots of simple directives, such as:

* hop on one foot;
* slither like a snake;
* zoom like an airplane;
* act like a gorilla;
* shake your arms and legs;

Simon should physically act out his own instructions as the other players mimic him. But when Simon gives a command *without* saying "Simon says" at the beginning, the other players should *not* obey those directions. Take turns playing the role of Simon, and enjoy trying to trip each other up by quickly issuing orders.

connection

Kids love playing Simon in this game because in real life they're always on the receiving end, having to obey their parents' commands. You can use this game to show your child that you *too* are called to obey someone: God.

Allow enough time to let your child enjoy being Simon for several rounds; then wrap up the game by being Simon and issuing lots of physically tiring commands. Finish with a command like, "Simon says sit on the floor and catch your breath!"

Sit down to rest with your child. As you do, briefly connect the game to real life by first emphasizing God's call on your life to fully obey his commands. Say something like, "Did you know that when God tells Mommy to do something, I'm supposed to totally obey him?" Invite your child to share ideas about things God wants you to do or obey. Emphasize *why* you obey God—because you love him. Also share about times when obedience feels difficult for you so your child can see that you understand how tough obedience can be.

Use the questions below to talk about how your child feels about obedience. Do your best to show empathy with the feelings and thoughts your child shares. Then wrap things up by reiterating an important point: Children are called to obey their parents (Eph. 6:1; Col. 3:20), and parents are called to obey God. Clarify that when your child is obeying what "Mommy says," he is being obedient to God.

exploration

You may want to ask your child questions like these:

* In real life, do you think it's easy or hard to obey commands and directions?
* What rules or commands in our house are easy for you to obey? Which are tough to obey?
* Why is it important for all of us to obey God?
* Why is it important for children to obey their parents?

79 sneaky sidewalk artists

Put a smile on someone's face with surprise messages of encouragement on their driveway.

supplies:
- sidewalk chalk
- camera
  (optional)

experience

Tell your child you're going to do something super-duper sneaky. First decide together on someone you want to encourage, such as a friend who is sick, a next-door neighbor, your child's teacher, or a relative. Then, with an exaggerated sense of sneakiness, drive with your child over to that person's house and spend about fifteen to thirty minutes decorating his driveway and sidewalks with pictures and words of encouragement. (If that person will be home, call ahead and warn him to stay inside and refrain from peeking out the window.)

When you're done, you may want to take a quick picture of your child by the artwork. Then hop in the car and zoom away.

connection

We're all selfish creatures; it can become very easy to go through each day completely focused on our own needs, our own hurts, our own desires. That's why God's Word tells us so many times to encourage each other! We need to be reminded many times to take our eyes off ourselves and put them squarely on others. Use this activity to train your child in the fine art of encouragement. He'll quickly discover how much joy results from helping someone else feel loved and inspired.

As you drive to your destination, share 1 Thessalonians 5:11 with your child: "Encourage one another and build each other up." Brainstorm together messages you can write and pictures you can draw that will really build up the person you're targeting.

Then when you're driving home afterward, affirm and encourage your child for what he just did. Say something like, "Our friend is going to feel so surprised and so happy when he sees what you drew. God is very happy about the way you just showed love and encouragement." Together say a short out-loud prayer (eyes open while you drive) for your friend, asking God to build him up and give him strength, hope, and joy in the Lord.

exploration

You may want to ask your child questions like these:

* How do you think our friend is going to feel when he sees the messages and drawings?
* What does it feel like to know you just encouraged someone else so much?
* Why do you think God wants us to encourage others?
* How can we do a better job of encouraging each other in our family? What are some ideas you have?

80 something new

*Watch chemistry in action to explore
how the Holy Spirit creates
something new in each of us.*

supplies:
- baking soda
- teaspoon measure
- an uninflated balloon
- funnel
- towel
- clean plastic soda bottle (20 oz. or smaller)
- vinegar
- electrical tape

experience

Together with your child, carefully set up your science experiment by following these steps:

1. Stretch out the balloon and affix the mouth of the balloon over the end of the funnel. Hold the funnel up and use your other hand to pull and stretch the balloon a bit while your child measures out three to four teaspoons of baking soda and dumps them into the funnel. Use your fingers to pull and prod the balloon as needed until all the baking soda has made its way into the balloon. Carefully take the balloon off the funnel and set it aside, keeping it upright so the baking soda doesn't spill out. Wash off the funnel and dry it with a towel.

2. Put the funnel into the top of the soda bottle and help your child fill the bottle about one-third full with vinegar.

3. Pinch or twist the end of the balloon, making sure *none* of the baking soda falls out. Then carefully affix the neck of the balloon onto the top of the bottle with the body of the balloon (filled with baking soda) hanging down to the side. Wrap electrical tape

around the base of the balloon several times to secure it in place on the bottle and to seal it tight.

Now, before you do the experiment, explain to your child what is going to happen. When the baking soda mixes with the vinegar, a chemical change takes place and something new is created: carbon dioxide gas.

Invite your child to lift up the balloon and shake it so that all the baking soda falls right into the vinegar in the bottle. Then sit back and watch what happens: Slowly the balloon will fill up with gas (carbon dioxide)! (If you hear air escaping, wrap your hand around the base of the balloon to hold it tightly against the bottle as gas fills the balloon.)

connection

This experiment can symbolize for us the work of the Holy Spirit in our lives: God's Spirit comes into our hearts, changes us, and creates new behaviors and values. In Galatians 5:22–23, these new traits are called the fruit of the Spirit. Share with your child the list of the Spirit's fruit and invite her to talk about ways she senses God creating some of these new values, actions, attitudes, and behaviors in her life.

The most important truth of this experience is to help your child get a sense that her God-honoring actions don't just come about by her own power or efforts. In fact, we don't have the ability to really change ourselves without God's help! Instead, help her to see that it is God's Spirit at work in her life, bubbling up, changing her, and creating new attitudes and actions that others can see.

exploration

You may want to ask your child questions like these:

* What are some ways you think God is changing you?
* What are some ways God's Spirit helps you show love (joy, peace, patience, kindness, goodness, faithfulness, self-control)?
* Are there any attitudes or actions in your life that you want God to change? How can I pray for you about that?

81 sweet words

Use bitter, sour, salty, and sweet tastes to help your child discover the power of his tongue.

supplies:
- a food that is bitter (such as very dark chocolate, coffee, or citrus peel)
- a food that is sour (such as a lemon slice)
- a food that is salty (such as a pinch of salt, saltine crackers, or salted peanuts)
- honey
- spoon
- glass of water

experience

Have you struggled with frustration over your child's words or tone of voice? Whether it's sassiness, rudeness, arguing, or meanness, you can help your child make a turn toward the positive power of words with a simple taste test.

Talk with your child about the four basic tastes we can sense with our tongue: bitterness, saltiness, sourness, and sweetness. (Some scientists add a fifth taste called "umami," which is related to savory, meaty, or fish-like flavors and is present in many Asian foods.) Invite your child to try a taste of bitter food, sour food, and salty food, cleansing his palate with water after each taste. Invite him to make faces and use words to describe each taste.

End with a delicious spoonful of sweet honey, again inviting your child to describe the honey's taste.

connection

If you feel that negative words or ways of speaking have been a problem in your home, you may want to talk briefly about this before you give your child the honey. Be very careful not to turn this into a disciplinary conversation; instead, just ask open-ended questions like, "How can words be bitter or sour?" or "What are some examples of bitter, sour ways of talking?" You could keep it lighthearted by acting out some examples with extremely exaggerated facial expressions and tones of voice. Do *not* refer directly to anything your child has said recently unless he does so himself.

When your child eats the honey, share this great Bible verse from the New Living Translation: "Kind words are like honey—sweet to the soul" (Prov. 16:24). Explain to your child that his tongue doesn't only have the power of taste, but it also has the power to affect others by the words he says. Talk together about choosing to use kind words when speaking with others. Then say some kind things directly to your child, telling him what you love about him.

exploration

You may want to ask your child questions like these:

* When have you heard people talk in a way that is bitter or sour or hurtful?
* What are some of the kindest, sweetest words you've heard lately?
* What are some of the kindest, sweetest words you've said lately?
* How can we do a better job of talking with kind, sweet words in our family?

82 three essential ingredients

Make a delicious treat to help your child focus on the important aspects of faithful living.

supplies:
- ingredients (see below)
- kitchen tools
- wax paper
- nonstick spray
- recipe card (or index card)
- pen

experience

Rice Krispies treats are easy to make and yummy to eat. Follow the instructions below to make this fun recipe with your child.

connection

In light of the gospel, we know that ultimately what God requires of us is that we have a faith relationship with Jesus. Unfortunately, many have made the error of stopping there. They focus so intently on personal faith that they overlook the other teachings in Scripture that describe the way God wants us to exhibit our faith through our actions and choices. One of the most direct and concise statements from God on this matter is Micah 6:8: "He has showed you, O man, what is good. And what does the LORD require of you? To act justly and to love mercy and to walk humbly with your God."

Rice Krispies treats have got about the shortest grocery list of any snack you'll make: just three basic ingredients! Use this cooking experience as a launching pad to talk with your child about the "three ingredients" God wants to see in the lives of his people.

As you sit down to eat your treats, ask your child, "How many ingredients were in these treats we made?" Then say, "In the Bible, God tells us about the three ingredients he wants to see in our lives." Share Micah 6:8 with your child and talk together about these three ingredients of godly living: justice, mercy, and humility. Define these words on your child's terms. For example, explain *justice* as doing the right thing and treating others fairly; describe *mercy* as caring about and showing love to people who are hurting; define *humility* as putting God in charge of your life instead of putting yourself in charge.

On your recipe card, have your child write "Recipe for Pleasing God" at the top. Then list the three ingredients of justice, mercy, and humility. Share ideas with each other for how a grown-up and a child could live out each of these traits in an average day. Then wrap up by praying together, asking God to grow these characteristics in your lives.

rice krispies treats

ingredients

- 5–6 c. Rice Krispies cereal (or a generic puffed rice cereal)
- 40 jumbo marshmallows (or 4 c. mini-marshmallows)
- 3 tbsp. butter

Using a wooden spoon, help your child melt the butter in a large pot on low heat. Meanwhile, prepare a 9 x 13 pan by spraying it with nonstick spray.

When the butter has melted, stir in the marshmallows until they've melted too. Turn off the heat and pour in the cereal. Quickly stir it into the marshmallow mixture until it's all coated.

Before things cool too much, dump the entire mixture into your prepared pan. Use a spatula to scrape out any extras sticking to your pot.

Use pieces of wax paper (to prevent the mixture from sticking to your hands) to press down the mixture until it's flat. Allow it to cool at room temperature. Cut it into squares and serve.

exploration

You may want to ask your child questions like these:

* What does it look like when a child lives justly?
* How can a kid like you show mercy?
* How can a child walk humbly with God?
* Think of someone you know who is a good example of a person who practices justice, mercy, or humility.
* Why do you think God wants his people to live this way?

top-secret smile-a-thon : **83**

*Turn running errands into a
secret mission of spreading joy.*

experience

You and your child are on a secret mission: to
spread joy and happiness to everyone you see as
you embark on a top-secret smile-a-thon! Visit a
public place together for errands (such as a mall,
grocery store, or library), but before you go inside

supplies:
• none

prep in the car by explaining the secret mission to your child. Basically,
your goal together is go about whatever business you have inside, but
as you do you'll also try to make eye contact with as many people as
you can and give them each a genuine, heartfelt smile.

connection

In our isolated and anonymous culture, sharing eye contact and
genuine smiles with others has become a thing of the past. But God
has called us to be a light of hope, kindness, and true joy in our
world. One very simple way we can do that is to communicate God's
love to others through facial expressions. Authentic, true smiles are
powerful things. Proverbs says "A cheerful look brings joy to the
heart" (Prov. 15:30). As you ready your child for your top-secret
smile-a-thon, share this verse with him, helping him to see that smiling

at others is more than just a superficial act—it can really touch someone's heart, especially someone who may feel hurt, lonely, or discouraged.

When you complete your smile-a-thon and are back in the car, share a smile with your child and tell him how proud you are of his efforts to share joy with others. Talk together about what it was like to give the gift of smiles to others and consider the effect it had on the smile recipients as well as on yourselves.

exploration

You may want to ask your child questions like these:

* Do you know anyone who smiles at you a lot (such as a teacher, grandparent, etc.)? What do those smiles "say" to you?
* When has a smile or a kind word really cheered you up or meant a lot to you?
* What was it like to smile so much in that store?
* How did people react to our smiles? Which people do you think we really cheered up?

when life gives you lemons 84

Help your child do some truly nonprofit work by running a free lemonade stand.

experience

It's a great entrepreneurial exercise for kids to run a neighborhood lemonade stand during the summer months. They can plan a "business," run it, and decide what to do with the profits.

But this time around, challenge your child to try a radical approach: giving the drinks away *for free*. Set up the stand, mix the lemonade, and create a poster together that can serve as the stand's sign. Write something like "Delicious Lemonade! Cost: FREE!"

Before your child begins giving the lemonade away, pray together, asking God to bless and bring joy to each person who receives a free cup of lemonade. Then encourage your child to give away each drink with a smile. If customers ask your child why she's giving the lemonade away instead of charging money, encourage her to say something like "It's just a free gift. I hope you enjoy it." If customers offer to donate money, have your child suggest that they instead donate it to a good cause on their own.

supplies:

- table
- stool
- paper cups
- pitcher
- ice
- water
- lemonade mix
- spoon
- piece of poster board
- markers
- masking tape

connection

"God loves a cheerful giver" (2 Cor. 9:7), and seeing the surprise on the faces of her customers will certainly bring your child great cheer! It's rare to get something for nothing in our culture, and your child's free gift will certainly have an impact on each person who receives it.

But perhaps it's even rarer to *do* something for nothing! It's just natural to work for some type of reward like money, approval, or praise. This experience of doing work without focusing on getting something in return will make a powerful impression on your child.

Further, it will be a spiritually refreshing time for her as she takes her focus off her own needs and wants. You may want to share Philippians 2:1–11 (especially verse 4) with your child and talk about what it means to focus on the needs of others. *The Message* puts the challenge of verse 4 in simple terms that can be a motto for your child's lemonade-stand service: "Forget yourselves long enough to lend a helping hand." Serving others, especially for free, provides us with a much-needed break from our incessant focus on self and trains us, bit by bit, to be more like Christ, who freely gave up everything for us.

exploration

You may want to ask your child questions like these:

* Do you think it was easy or hard to "work" for free? Why?
* What did you like about giving away lemonade for free?
* Who seemed most surprised that the drinks were free?
* How do you think getting a free drink made your customers feel?

faith-filled moments finder

Use these lists and categories to find just the right
experience to share with your child today.

Cooking Projects and Stuff to Eat
Asleep on the Hay (Moment 44)
Empty Inside (Moment 2)
Fishers of People (Moment 46)
Fruit (of the Spirit) Salad (Moment 47)
Gobbling Up Monsters (Moment 3)
It's Empty! (Moment 50)
Peeled Away (Moment 11)
Pretzel Prayer (Moment 37)
Sweet Words (Moment 81)
Three Essential Ingredients (Moment 82)
White (and Yummy) as Snow (Moment 63)
Yummy Family Portrait (Moment 21)

Games and Playtime
A to Z Thanks (Moment 22)
And the Winner Is . . . (Moment 43)
Defensive Moves (Moment 27)
Glow-Stick Tag (Moment 70)
Goal! (Moment 48)
God's Love Is Like These (Moment 4)
Keep in Step (Moment 32)
Mystery Drive (Moment 34)
Simon Says (Moment 78)
Tic-Tac-Toe, Where Will You Go? (Moment 14)
True Treasure Hunt, The (Moment 61)
What Are You Seeking? (Moment 42)
You Are My Hiding Place (Moment 18)

Crafts and Hands-On Projects
A Twist, a Tie . . . a Masterpiece! (Moment 15)
Color Prayers (Moment 1)

Destination: God's Ear (Moment 28)
Divine Valentines (Moment 66)
God Rocks! (Moment 49)
Grooming Generosity (Moment 71)
Like a Tree (Moment 52)
More Than Pen Pals (Moment 72)
Pass the Peas . . . and Pray for the World
   (Moment 74)
Pictures of Praise (Moment 54)
Prayer Portrait (Moment 36)
Quite a Kingdom (Moment 55)
Reduce, Reuse, Recycle (Moment 76)
Salty Special Effects (Moment 56)
Send a Shoebox (Moment 77)
Snuggle Up (Moment 12)

Science Projects and Kid-Friendly Chemistry
Bright as New (Moment 25)
Bubble Power (Moment 45)
Connected (Moment 26)
Crystal-Clear Evidence (Moment 65)
Filled Up (Moment 29)
God's Recycling Business (Moment 5)
Hidden-Away Hope (Moment 6)
In the Light (Moment 30)
Jesus' Touch (Moment 51)
Overflowing Joy (Moment 35)
Peace Bottle (Moment 10)
Soak Up the Good Stuff (Moment 59)
Something New (Moment 80)
Sweet Words (Moment 81)
Up-Close Examination (Moment 41)

Family Outings

Bird-Watching and God-Listening (Moment 23)
Life on the Farm (Moment 33)
Life's Ups and Downs (Moment 8)
Like a Tree (Moment 52)
Made by the Master Artist (Moment 9)
Mystery Drive (Moment 34)
One-Buck-Giveaway Challenge, The
  (Moment 73)
Sneaky Sidewalk Artists (Moment 79)
Top-Secret Smile-A-Thon (Moment 83)

No Supplies Needed (or Hardly Any!)

A to Z Thanks (Moment 22)
An Invisible (Not Imaginary) Friend
  (Moment 31)
Big-Time Service (Moment 64)
Breathe In, Breathe Out (Moment 24)
Destination: God's Ear (Moment 28)
Get One, Give One (Moment 68)
Is God Crying? (Moment 7)
Plaid and Polka-Dots? (Moment 75)
Silent Sunrise (Moment 39)
Simon Says (Moment 78)
Top-Secret Smile-A-Thon (Moment 83)
TV Turn-Off Week (Moment 40)
You Are My Hiding Place (Moment 18)
Your Inner Compass (Moment 20)

Warm Weather Outdoor Fun

Bird-Watching and God-Listening (Moment 23)
Filled Up (Moment 29)
Giveaway Garden (Moment 69)
Glow-Stick Tag (Moment 70)
Goal! (Moment 48)
Life's Ups and Downs (Moment 8)
Like a Tree (Moment 52)
Overflowing Joy (Moment 35)
Pictures of Praise (Moment 54)
Pulling Soul-Weeds (Moment 38)
Setting Up Camp (Moment 57)
Simon Says (Moment 78)
Soaring Hope (Moment 13)
Star Light, Star Bright (Moment 60)
When Life Gives You Lemons (Moment 84)
Worm Hunt (Moment 17)
You Are My Hiding Place (Moment 18)
Your Inner Compass (Moment 20)

Cold Weather Fun

Hidden-Away Hope (Moment 6)
Keep in Step (Moment 32)
Silent Sunrise (Moment 39)
White (and Yummy) as Snow (Moment 63)

Indoor Fun

And the Winner Is . . . (Moment 43)
Big-Time Service (Moment 64)
Color Prayers (Moment 1)
Is God Crying? (Moment 7)
More Than Pen Pals (Moment 72)
Pass the Peas . . . and Pray for the World
  (Moment 74)
Quite a Kingdom (Moment 55)
Simon Says (Moment 78)
Sing a New (Old) Song (Moment 58)
Tic-Tac-Toe, Where Will You Go? (Moment 14)
True Treasure Hunt, The (Moment 61)
Ultimate Fort, The (Moment 16)
Up-Close Examination (Moment 41)
You Are My Hiding Place (Moment 18)
You Won't See *That* at the Zoo! (Moment 19)

Perfect for the Littlest Ones (Toddlers and Younger)

And the Winner Is . . . (Moment 43)
Big-Time Service (Moment 64)
Gobbling Up Monsters (Moment 3)
Is God Crying? (Moment 7)
It's Empty! (Moment 50)
Peeled Away (Moment 11)
Quite a Kingdom (Moment 55)
Sing a New (Old) Song (Moment 58)
Top-Secret Smile-A-Thon (Moment 83)

Great for Older Kids (Elementary School Age)

A Twist, a Tie . . . a Masterpiece! (Moment 15)
Crystal-Clear Evidence (Moment 65)
Defensive Moves (Moment 27)
Do-Good Dates (Moment 67)
Empty Inside (Moment 2)
Glow-Stick Tag (Moment 70)
Made by the Master Artist (Moment 9)
Pictures of Praise (Moment 54)
Setting Up Camp (Moment 57)
Snuggle Up (Moment 12)
Something New (Moment 80)
Star Light, Star Bright (Moment 60)

Ideas for the Holidays

Asleep on the Hay (Advent or Christmas)
  (Moment 44)
Divine Valentines (February or October for
  Clergy Appreciation month) (Moment 66)
It's Empty! (Easter) (Moment 50)
Pretzel Prayer (Lent or Easter) (Moment 37)
Send a Shoebox (Thanksgiving or Christmas)
  (Moment 77)